EVERY LITTLE THING YOU DO IS MAGIC

AN INTERACTIVE GUIDE TO TAROT, RITUAL, AND PERSONAL GROWTH

CALLIE LITTLE *and* MOOREA SEAL

Clarkson Potter/Publishers
New York, New York

CONTENTS

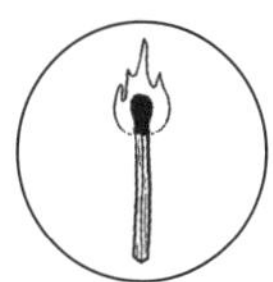   

THE MAJOR ARCANA

THE MINOR ARCANA

INTRODUCTION

Within each of us is the hero and the guide of our own magical journey. They show up in mundane or quiet ways—when our gut tells us to do something kind, when we make a right turn instead of a left, when we reflect on a hard decision made and say, *I am proud of my choices despite any hardship.* Perhaps you call this intuition, or your moral compass, or even a higher power. No matter how you imagine your inner self, that hero is part of you. You are the being who wakes up each day and makes this life what it is. What a miracle! We, the authors of the book in your hands, truly believe that *Every Little Thing You Do Is Magic.*

Through the practice of tarot, all people, regardless of belief system or heritage, can access their inner guide. The narrative sequence of the tarot begins, as we do in life, with the Fool—a clear-eyed youth ready to take on the world, caution be damned! It can be challenging to take that leap off a ledge and into the unknown, whether in real life or with something as old and mysterious as these cards. We understand the intimidation that may come with buying your first deck (and let us just clear something up right now: You do *not* have to be gifted your first deck! That is a safeguarding myth from times past). We also know that it's hard to commit to something new, and easy to fall into a rut with any practice in life.

It's easy to ignore the call to go inward. So many of us have been raised to abandon ourselves in favor of people-pleasing. And for many the world over, the COVID-19 pandemic was a wake-up call on a profound level. It forced us to confront our many inner selves. The hermitude of social distancing provided a new appreciation for our communities and a forced lesson in seeking guidance from within. This shadow work is the most integral piece of radical self-love. As we continue to navigate the pandemic's waves along with our shadow selves, we've noticed that the desire for purpose, a sense of belonging, and understanding is at an all-time high. This book is our community offering: a resource and support system for the exploration and validation of self—one that can be used throughout a lifetime, come what may.

Our traditional education system teaches people to develop intellectual knowledge, yet grossly avoids the development of an individual's inner well-being, self-acceptance, and most profoundly, one's intuition. For seekers, theories on the eternal question of "Who am I?" can be found in the practice of tarot. We've provided clear, easy-to-understand guidance in these pages so that an absolute beginner can start reading tarot the same day they open this workbook or our intuitively crafted deck and guidebook. Likewise, we've endeavored to ensure that even the most experienced tarot reader will discover new insights and fresh inspiration within these pages.

Inherent to the centuries-old tradition of tarot is the cultivation of trust in the self. Tarot challenges us to be mindful about how we show up for ourselves, asking us to turn *habits* into mindful *rituals*, to see the beauty in everyday living. In this workbook, you will find practical and inspiring tools to hold yourself gently, with awareness, accountability, and honesty. The habits that rule our daily lives, whether we are conscious of them or not, can direct us away from our inner knowing if we are not aware of our self-sabotaging behaviors. Herein, we'll walk you through tarot and divinatory practices and show you how to practice self-awareness, strengthen self-trust, and develop your intuition. You are being given a big, juicy tool kit to gain a deeper understanding of the self you've been longing for. Together, we (you + us!) are co-creators of this workbook, a reference and your living encyclopedia of intuition.

This is your book. Use it as *you* see fit. Cover the pages in notes and drawings, tape in pages from other texts. Rip it apart and turn it into something else if you so desire! Whatever you need this book to be, make it so. Don't be afraid to get messy. Play around. Get creative. Allow curiosity to sit beside you.

Now take a few deep breaths and get comfortable—we're about to make magic together.

A LETTER FROM CALLIE LITTLE

Tarot has been on the periphery of my life since before I can remember. My late mother was a deeply spiritual person who dabbled in various religious and esoteric practices, and I followed in her footsteps as soon as I could walk. Growing up in my father's Southern Baptist family also meant that I was familiar with the expectations of more conventional, socially accepted belief systems. I attended church, sang hymns in the choir, and ate my weight in potluck ambrosia salad. At night, though, I'd curl up beneath my sheets with a flashlight and a book from my mother's shelf. I'd read volumes on the topics of astral travel, developing psychic "powers," reading auras, contacting ghosts . . . I had one foot in the doorway of Christianity and the other in the occult. While it may seem as if these two realms are in opposition to each other, I believe they can—and do—exist in harmony.

THERE IS NOTHING UNHOLY ABOUT ANYTHING THAT MAKES US FEEL MORE CONNECTED TO THE DIVINE.

While I am no longer connected to my family of origin, I still hold these early memories of self-exploration close to my heart. Today I identify as pagan; I believe in ancient spiritual practices like honoring the earth via the Wheel of the Year—a seasonally charged calendar with traditions like baking bread, appreciating ancestors, and caring for the land. I also identify as a witch, which means that I believe my thoughts and actions can work in tandem to create change in both my personal world and the greater collective. This doesn't mean that I wave around a wand to clean my house (no matter how much I wish it worked like that), nor do I "hex" anyone. It just means that I spend time considering what I have to offer in my lifetime, what I hope to accomplish and receive, and I create intentional rituals as initiations for these things to come to fruition. A common example of witchcraft that most people in the Western world might understand is blowing out the candles on a birthday cake: You make a wish, blow out the flame of last year in celebration of the new one to come, and then share the sweetness of this intention with your loved ones. There's nothing evil within this ritual, just tradition, hopes, dreams, and community. Connection. This is the basis of magic.

To me, tarot is an extension of my connection to the unseeable parts of life. I'm able to tap into my intuitive voice, the wisdom that lives beneath the surface of my consciousness, and that which electrifies the universe. I hope that this interactive guide to tarot puts you deeply in touch with yourself, the world around you, and the times that both have passed and are to come.

Wishing you magic,

Callie Little

CALLIE LITTLE (She/They)

A LETTER FROM **MOOREA SEAL**

I was a deeply religious, spiritual, and cerebral child, one of those kids often called "wise beyond their years" or "an old soul," always seeking the meaning to my existence. I was not a playful or charming kid—at least in a way the outside world could understand. I grew up in a home where the exploration of religions, spiritual paths, and artistic practices was highly encouraged. My dad is a retired Episcopalian priest and Buddhist teacher, and my mom a writer and artist. Both are analytical, deep souls and seekers of greater knowledge. Like my parents, I'm a researcher and artist at heart, a curious being who studies myself and others to hone my own intuition and empathy. Seeking and creating resources for self-soothing are core to my existence.

Like many in my family before me, I am a sensitive spirit, and depression and anxiety have been lifelong challenges and major occupiers of my attention. I'm hyper in tune with animals, people, and the world around me and often feel overwhelmed with energetic awareness. For much of my life, this caused me to live in a constant state of fight-or-flight and overstimulation. It wasn't until I found the practice of tarot in my mid-twenties that I finally learned how to channel energy in a way that felt supportive to my well-being.

I have no attachments to any particular religions. My spiritual practice is centered in tarot, art, list-making, and a connection to nature; a life devoted to mental, emotional, spiritual, and physical well-being. My morning meditation is to ask an open-ended question, pull a tarot card, and spend time in contemplation with the card's art and wisdom from tarot readers of the past and present. As a diagnosed-late-in-life Autistic person—and just as a *person*—finding modes for regulating energy and emotion is essential for existing in a buzzing world. If you identify as highly sensitive, an empath, or neurodivergent in any way, I'm sure you can relate. The world at large demands us to show up as cogs in a machine, yet there is something inside of us that asks, *Is this really it? Can't there be more meaning to my life?* This book and our accompanying tarot deck are here to say *yes*. Tarot is here to support you in seeking and defining what *your* life is meant to be.

I hope that you find a deeper sense of understanding and acceptance of yourself and your needs as your relationship with tarot develops. You are meant to meet the healer that already lives within you, and through self-inquiry, you will find more ease and meaning to your days. Through always remaining curious and open to new learning, we create purpose in our existence.

MAY YOUR INWARD JOURNEY BE A LIFELONG JOY OF FOREVER GREETING THE MANY FACETS OF YOU.

Wishing you peace,

Moorea Seal

MOOREA SEAL (She/They)

A BRIEF HISTORY OF TAROT

We believe in knowing where our practices come from to ensure we are not appropriating closed rituals of cultures outside our own. Fortunately for all of us, tarot has an eclectic history that is as much a rich tapestry of cultures as our world is. Here is what we know about the history of tarot—though you could probably spend a lifetime learning about this ever-changing practice.

It's difficult to find hard evidence of where myth and fact separate and come together, but we can assume that the search for secret, inner wisdom has been a human pursuit for thousands of years, as evidenced by the existence of many secret societies and religions, timeless philosophical quandaries, and records of self-reflection. And cartomancy, the reading of cards for divination and the curiosity of self, has likely been around even before its first documentation in the fifteenth century.

Today, you can find hundreds of thousands of people from all walks of life using tarot for personal use. What was once associated with secret societies and hidden wisdom has become accessible to all who seek a deeper knowing of the self and the world around them.

FOURTEENTH CENTURY

A grand conference of Kabbalists and other masters, which many scholars believe was the root of the ritualistic journey of the tarot, takes place in Morocco.

FIFTEENTH CENTURY

The Visconti-Sforza deck, painted by Bonifacio Bembo for the influential Visconti family of Milan, is the earliest evidence of a classic deck of playing cards that Italians called tarocchi.

EIGHTEENTH CENTURY

The French occultist Antoine Court de Gébelin makes the claim that tarot originated from the Book of Thoth. *His fellow occultist Etteilla pioneers an interpretation concept for tarot cards around 1783. He is influenced by Marie Anne Lenormand, a divination professional, and adapts her form of card-reading to the reading of tarot cards.*

NINETEENTH CENTURY

The poet, author, and esoteric Éliphas Lévi creates the Tarot of Marseilles deck; it is noted as the first deck used specifically for occult purposes.

THE KEYS TO THE TAROT

To fully understand the meaning of each card and the key life lesson it represents, we must look at all its parts. We consider symbology, numerology, and intuition to be the three crucial keys to the tarot.

SYMBOLOGY

Symbology is the visual language of the tarot. Symbolism can be found everywhere, from the animals that cross our paths to what we see in dreams and even in the logos on our clothing. In the everyday shuffle of life, we see most things as rather ordinary, everyday occurrences. But when we pay attention to what's happening around us—by examining our experience and the personal connections we have to the world around us—these mundanities can all transform into something more magical.

When reading the tarot, regardless of the deck you use, you'll see many symbols. Some may be universal symbols that are easily identified with similar understanding across the board. Others are more niche, and some will be entirely personal. In one of Callie's favorite decks, for example, *The Lioness Oracle Tarot* by Alejandra Luisa León, roses, space, and big cats are persistent themes. Most people would probably agree that a lion has quite a different meaning when compared to a tabby kitten. If you're a historian, you might know that in the Victorian language of flowers, roses of different colors mean different things. You could also have a personal anecdote about an image and that would be equally important to your reading. If you see an owl on a card, for example, and it reminds you of a favorite T-shirt from your childhood, use that insight. What might that symbol mean in your life? Perhaps the card is related to your past or an inner child. Maybe it's hinting at nostalgia, or something as simple as the clothing you're currently wearing.

In one of Moorea's favorite decks, *The Wild Unknown* by Kim Krans, black-and-white illustrations are contrasted by boldly saturated rainbows. These two spectrums of color tell a story all their own: The black and white might speak to the simplicity of certain life lessons and the technicolor scope of the human experience. A darkly lined card may allude to the heavy, impending nature of depression, while bright yellow rays may indicate a time of great warmth and, well, brightness.

Each deck has its own language and each will speak to you differently. When we're paying attention to and connecting with ourselves all the way from the top of our minds down into the depths of our intuition, working with your deck should feel like a conversation with a trusted friend. And, in our opinion, that relationship is kind of the most important part.

TWENTIETH CENTURY

The Rider-Waite-Smith deck is published in 1909. The collaboration between the artist and occultist Pamela Colman Smith and the academic and mystic A. E. Waite is influenced by the Hermetic Order of the Golden Dawn, friends of Smith's, and Éliphas Lévi's interpretation of tarot. A few decades later, Aleister Crowley and Lady Frieda Harris publish the Thoth Tarot.

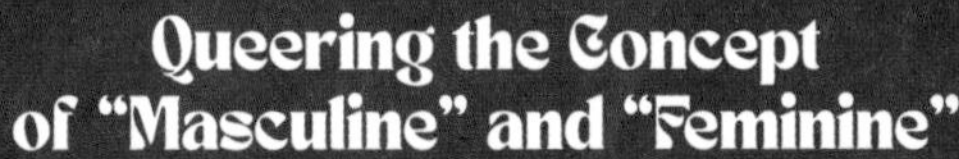

Queering the Concept of "Masculine" and "Feminine"

We try to limit the usage of these terms in our work, as they have been falsely and inappropriately equated with gender as our language has evolved. Below is an offering to inclusively reframe the original intent behind these words to serve a broader, more diverse audience. We hope this helps you unlock the closet of language used in many traditional tarot texts, especially the older (and often incredibly useful) guides out there.

MASCULINITY *or masculine energy encompasses the forthright or direct energies in the universe. For example, the Sun (both the card and the star itself) is considered "masculine," but not because it is related to men in any way. The sun is a provider of light, fire, warmth—it pours its energy into the universe. The intensity of the sun is an example of traditional masculinity but can also be understood as an energy of providing, giving, and igniting.*

FEMININITY *or feminine energy is a term for receptive and indirect energies in the universe. It's not inherently about women. For example, the Moon can be related to reflections—as the moon reflects the sun's light, for example—amplifying that which is being projected onto it. This symbol represents an energy that has more going on beneath the surface than what might be visible to the outside world. Like the moon, feminine energy often receives projections, but it also has a mysterious, unseen nature.*

Why Our Court Cards Have New Names

If you have used other tarot decks, you've probably seen court cards labeled as Page, Knight, Queen, and King. We are here to shake up the inherent biases in the traditional world of the royal courts. In our tarot world, all people are welcome and given the opportunity to rise. For this reason, we have renamed our court cards:

THE APPRENTICE (TRADITIONALLY TITLED THE PAGE): *Someone in pursuit of growth or gaining new opportunities for educational progress. They have quite a way to go before becoming masters of their own wisdom, influence, and skill.*

THE CHAMPION (TRADITIONALLY TITLED THE KNIGHT): *Someone who has been through great training and has likely risen in rank with much success. They've been lauded externally but have yet to truly embody inward mastery of the self.*

THE ORACLE (TRADITIONALLY TITLED THE QUEEN): *Someone who has done internal work to seek deep wisdom. They have been on a vision quest and will soon reenter the physical world to commune with those who have also been to the other side.*

THE ELDER (TRADITIONALLY TITLED THE KING): *A peaceful and powerful sage who has lived a full life, adventured inward and out, and communed with others from a variety of world perspectives. They have found enlightenment and are willing to share wisdom to uplift others.*

—✱—

The suits of tarot's Minor Arcana represent the earth's elements (water, fire, earth, and air) and four of the most integral pillars of life as we know it—emotions, action, physical life, and thought. While the Major Arcana speaks to some of life's greatest initiations and touchstones, the Minors speak to the little things in life that make up those greater pictures.

WANDS

The suit of Wands relates to the element of fire and corresponds to the astrological signs Aries, Leo, and Sagittarius. This is the suit of action, energy, and personal passion. When you see fire show up on a card as wands, matchsticks, volcanoes erupting, or anything reminding you of flames, consider how this might connect to your own energy. What are you radiating?

CUPS

The suit of Cups relates to the element of water and corresponds to the astrological signs Cancer, Scorpio, and Pisces. This is the suit of emotion. When you see water show up on a card in any form—through a cup, a fish, a rain cloud, or something else that makes you think of liquid—pay attention. How might this symbol relate to your own emotional center?

SWORDS

The suit of Swords relates to the element of air and corresponds to the astrological signs Gemini, Libra, and Aquarius. This is the suit of imagination, intellect, and all things to do with the mind. When swords, smoke, clouds, wind, balloons, or anything that reminds you of breath show up in your reading, this is elemental air. Pay attention to these cards when it comes to belief systems, analyzations, learned thinking, and the conscious self. Are your thought patterns serving you?

PENTACLES

The suit of Pentacles, also known as Coins, relates to the element of earth and corresponds to the astrological signs Taurus, Virgo, and Capricorn. This is the suit of home, hearth, and money. Through the lens of mental health support, Moorea also likes to think of Pentacles as a reflection of behavior. Whenever earth shows up in your reading through coins, pentacles, or other representations of money, landscapes, planets, or anything that roots us to this plane of existence, take note. These cards are connected to your finances, home life, stability, and your outward behavior. What are you investing in?

NUMEROLOGY

Numbers hint at the spirit behind a card, poking at grander themes beyond our individual experience, making them an important layer for any tarot reading. While intuition informs our personal interpretation of each card, numerology provides distinct instruction on how to connect with tarot.

We've left a blank space for you to add your own notes and interpretations for each number. It's okay if nothing comes to mind at first—come back to these pages again and again. You can always fill in the blanks later as you get to know each number better.

ONE, 1, I, ACE The Alpha is at the forefront of all that is to come. This first number represents the individual, our divinity as both earthly and spiritual beings, creativity, and power. In the tarot, this shows up as the ace of each suit.

When I think of the number 1, I think of ______________________________

TWO, 2, II This dynamic duo represents unity between us and what is considered "the other." It is the conscious and subconscious, darkness and light, day and night, and all dualities in the universe. With the emergence of two, we introduce something outside ourselves into the fold.

When I think of the number 2, I think of ______________________________

THREE, 3, III A trio of energies comes together in the number three and reminds us of classic trios such as mind, body, and spirit; mother, father, and child; or perhaps the earth, a seed, and its plant. Trios tend to balance personal growth with building others up to something that can't be accomplished as individuals or pairs.

When I think of the number 3, I think of ______________________________

FOUR, 4, IV Fours represent structure, reason, and logic, asking us to consider how we are simultaneously a perfect, divine spirit (an individual, 1) in relationship to all that is within and outside of us (a pair, 2), who can expand through the expression of mind, body, and spirit (a trio, 3). This number is the realization and expression of our spirit and potential.

When I think of the number 4, I think of ______________________________

FIVE, 5, V Fives evoke instability. We also see five within the sacred pentacle—a five-pointed star representing the four elements and the fifth: spirit. The true nature of life and the universe *is* chaos (and creativity, which is perhaps not a different thing at all), so there's no need to fear; just pay attention to the fives' slippery, shifting nature.

When I think of the number 5, I think of ______________________________

SIX, 6, VI Six is typically associated with the planet Venus and the "feminine" spirit (see "Queering the Concept of 'Masculine' and 'Feminine'" on page 10). It is a number of sensuality, acceptance, and harmony. When we align our mind, body, and soul (3), and amplify (multiply) that spirit in conjunction with others (2), we find 3 x 2 = 6.

When I think of the number 6, I think of ______________________________

SEVEN, 7, VII A very holy number relating to the Sabbath, the day of rest and spiritual contemplation. Seven deadly sins, the lucky number seven . . . this number is all about wisdom and spiritual enlightenment. When we rest, nourish ourselves, and prioritize self-awareness, wouldn't you say our chances of good luck are greatly increased?

When I think of the number 7, I think of ______________________________

EIGHT, 8, VIII Turn the eight on its side and you'll see both the symbol for infinity and a minimalist representation of the scales of justice. This number relates to balance, judgment, and regeneration. When this number comes up, ask yourself what isn't working, honor it with a loving goodbye, and shed that old skin, those old beliefs and patterns to make space for something new.

When I think of the number 8, I think of ______________________________

NINE, 9, IX What a magical number. When multiplied by any other, the nine generates numbers that can be added up to become itself again: 9 x 2 = 18 and 1 + 8 = 9, and so on. This is an indicator of completion. Nine is often a solitary number and can be related to study, advancement of skills, and the cultivation of the relationship to oneself.

When I think of the number 9, I think of ______________________________

TEN, 10, X Ten's one and zero are the individual and the spirit, respectively. A ten indicates an achievement of full potential: a journey that has reached completion. This completion can be positive (see the Ten of Pentacles, page 161) or challenging (see the Ten of Swords, page 136). Now is the time to rest or celebrate before moving toward the next journey.

When I think of the number 10, I think of ______________________________

INTUITION

Intuition is not a mystical, untouchable force reserved only for the most magical thinkers. It's the hair that stands at the back of our neck in the quiet dark; the pit in our stomach when a beloved says, "We need to talk"; the smell of winter's hollow cold that means snow is on the way. Intuition is the subconscious knowledge that connects dots we don't notice on a surface level; it often works separately from our conscious mind.

Our ancestors utilized intuition to simply survive—it was important to notice the color of the sky, the direction of the wind, if the salmon were late that year . . . These signals from the world live all around us and, if we pay attention, we're able to understand a new language. The language of living.

> "INTUITION AND CONCEPTS CONSTITUTE . . . THE ELEMENTS OF ALL OUR KNOWLEDGE, SO THAT NEITHER CONCEPTS WITHOUT AN INTUITION IN SOME WAY CORRESPONDING TO THEM, NOR INTUITION WITHOUT CONCEPTS, CAN YIELD KNOWLEDGE."
>
> —**IMMANUEL KANT (1724–1804),** *philosopher, ethicist, teacher*

There are many ways to think of your intuition. Some might identify intuition as survival instincts or the ability to identify patterns, while others might feel the subtle guidance of a guardian spirit or the echoes of ancestors' wisdom. You might feel something completely different, or perhaps you feel that *all* of this is true for you. Whatever role your intuition occupies in your life is valid. As you walk the hero's journey of the tarot, you'll need to access your intuition.

ARCHETYPES, THE HERO'S JOURNEY, AND THE FOOL'S JOURNEY

Consider the stories of religious figures such as Jesus Christ and Mohammed, or a fairy tale like Cinderella, and you will see the hero's journey has been at play in storytelling for thousands of years. First named by the American mythologist Joseph Campbell in his book *The Hero with a Thousand Faces* (1949), the hero's journey lays a template for the story of an excitable young person in search of adventure. They face physical danger, intellectual challenges, emotional heartaches, and a breaking of the ego. They meet guides and teachers along the way, and they must face their ultimate battle alone. The hero returns home triumphant and, more important, aged and enlightened.

This narrative arc plays out in the Major Arcana and is often called the Fool's Journey. On closer inspection, the tarot offers a unique mirroring of the traditional hero's tale. While the hero's journey is a linear path that cycles back to the beginning after completion, the Fool's Journey can loop within itself, reverse and flip and challenge our notion of what it means to grow up or move forward. Yes, the Major Arcana takes a similar path to the hero's journey, but it is then supplemented by the four suits—the Minor Arcana—illuminating their own facets of humanity through Wands (energy), Cups (emotion), Swords (intellect), Pentacles (the physical).

The hero's journey and the Fool's Journey contain many parallels, but with the shuffling of tarot cards you are released from predictable, step-by-step growth and gifted with an awareness of the complexity of humanity. It moves in and out, backwards, forward, embodies one card, two, or many at once, all along the Fool's Journey.

As in life, there are archetypes in the tarot that build upon each other in distinct progression, just as a child grows to an adolescent and, eventually, an adult. The High Priestess, for example, would not hold wisdom without having first been through the growth of the playful Fool and the trickster Magician. It helps to know the overarching progression of the tarot, but remember, none of us follows a truly linear path—we are destined to bounce around in our accrual of wisdom. Each of us weaves a unique path of growth, revisiting some moments, skipping others, and deepening those periods in life that feel like true moments of resonance with our souls. You are a one-of-a-kind creature, and the cards will help you navigate your journey with more clarity, awareness, and imagination.

Our lifelong hero's journey begins with the Fool (card 0, our birth) and ends with the World (card XXI, our transcendence from this life to whatever comes next). Throughout the course of our lives, we live this cycle on repeat, in its many iterations, large and small, again and again. As we learn the lessons each archetype or experience offers, we are the Fool anew. Each card prompts its own hero's journey.

As you utilize this book and create your own association with the cards, you can use the space below to consider your personal journeys—the lifelong seeking of attainment and the smaller journeys that make us so vividly, beautifully, painfully human. Write down plot points from your life that connect to each card in the Major Arcana, to give greater depth to your interpretation of each card. By identifying the lessons of our past, we are less likely to repeat the same mistakes and more likely to integrate our learnings in the future.

THE FOOL:

THE MAGICIAN:

THE HIGH PRIESTESS:

THE EMPRESS:

THE EMPEROR:

THE HIEROPHANT:

THE LOVERS:

THE CHARIOT:

STRENGTH:

THE HERMIT:

THE WHEEL OF FORTUNE:

JUSTICE:

THE HANGED ONE:

DEATH:

Re-mything Your Journey

Re-mything is the process of imagining our life's story in creative ways, seeing ourselves through a new, more universal lens. While sometimes we may feel as if no one truly understands us at our core, we know that many people can easily understand Greek myths, classic fairy tales, and other forms of storytelling. Re-mything your story connects you to the world at large.

If you imagine your life as a tale full of symbolism and great lessons, who would you be? You may identify with an archetype from the tarot, or you might find yourself in ancient mythology, folklore, or religious parables. What archetypes do you identify with? What characters do you see yourself in? What characters and archetypes do you wish you saw yourself in? When you think of the greatest lessons you've learned in life so far, what comes to mind? Look to the tarot for ideas and give your personal obstacles a name. Let them become a force to interact with.

Finally, create your myth. Tell a story with a beginning, middle, and ending. What is your hero's journey?

TEMPERANCE: ______________________

THE MOON: ______________________

THE DEVIL: ______________________

THE SUN: ______________________

THE TOWER: ______________________

JUDGMENT: ______________________

THE STAR: ______________________

THE WORLD: ______________________

CARD PULLS AND SPREADS

As you develop your practice and put your newfound knowledge to use, you may discover rituals and specific card pulls that work well for you. Try the spreads below and consider making a list of your favorite pulls and questions, or brainstorm your own ideas.

Remember: Readings are never instructions on how to live your life or predictions of the future. Only you can choose your path—the Major and Minor Arcana are just here to help light the way.

DAILY WISDOM

Touching your cards each day will help you build a relationship to the practice of tarot, your intuition, and devotion. Keep a deck at your bedside, your desk, the glove compartment in your car, or coffee table—wherever it makes the most sense. Ask an open-ended question, something like, "what do I need to know to support myself well today," pull a card, and receive what the card has to offer. It may provide a bit of advice, a mentor, a whisper in your ear . . . Let yourself *feel* from the card and be honest with yourself. If you feel confused or disconnected from the card, or you need clarity on its message, consider pulling a second card.

PAST, PRESENT, FUTURE

Consider this spread the little red X that reads "YOU ARE HERE" on the map of your life. This classic three-card draw can be helpful for determining the path ahead. The past card can help you see lessons you've learned (or those that may need repeating). The present will show where you are now, in correlation with the first card. The future card shows where you're headed—where you might end up if you continue on the path ahead as you currently plan. Remember, the cards do not assign your fate.

CALLING FORTH MENTORSHIP

When you're in need of a guiding light, ask the cards for assistance. Shuffle your deck and imagine a blank space that fresh energy can fill. You might envision a person whose features are just out of focus. Pull one card and as you read its description, allow this visualization to take the shape of an imagined mentor. Display your card somewhere accessible as a reminder of this guide throughout your day.

THEME, MESSAGE, GUIDE

Try this three-card spread when you are feeling stuck or uninspired. This layout, created by the American witch Amanda Yates Garcia (AKA the Oracle of LA), is great if you are unsure what to ask but want to open yourself up to the wisdom of the universe. The first card, the theme, illustrates the context of your reading. The second card, the message, is the lesson seeking understanding and action. Finally, the guide is the energy necessary to accomplish what must be done. It may be the ingredient that has been missing all along!

UNSEEN OBSTACLES

If you just cannot figure out what is getting in the way of your desired outcomes, ask the cards to help you see what you've overlooked. For readers who tend to think in extremes, we recommend setting your biases aside and allowing the intention of the card pulled to shine through. When we are aware of our own biases and blockages, we can overcome them and find balance.

ME, YOU, US

A simple reading for any pair. You might use this reading to help figure out a conflict with a family member or to see how you might work with a potential romantic partner. Be mindful of your desired outcome and expectations before pulling these cards—remain open to possibility and hold on to neutrality; when we hope for a certain result, we may influence the way we read into things. Take some deep, cleansing breaths and repeat this affirmation:

I AM MYSELF, NOTHING MORE. YOU ARE YOURSELF, NOTHING MORE. TOGETHER WE ARE OURSELVES.

The Major Arcana

INTRODUCTION TO THE MAJORS

CONSIDER WHAT THESE CARDS WOULD LOOK LIKE IN YOUR MIND: *a gentle, firm hand on your shoulder encouraging you through some of life's biggest moments; a match to light the fire underfoot; a wise, beloved voice saying,* You can do it. *What archetypal title would you assign to each of these cards if they were yet unnamed?*

The Majors are revelations. The twenty-two cards of the Major Arcana are often viewed as the secrets that unlock the mysteries of the universe. Each card represents a major theme or archetype in the shared human experience, whether physical, spiritual, psychological, or emotional—often, the cards encompass it all.

Often called the Fool's Journey, the Major Arcana puts shared human characteristics on display alongside common characters or situations we may greet in life, as well as life's challenges, life's triumphs, and every in-between. The art within each card is designed to help you transform the abstract into something concrete in your mind, led by your unique perspective. When the art of a tarot deck melds with the art of your own life's journey, *that* is where a tarot reading really takes place.

We encourage you to read beyond the title of each card and find your own intuitive meaning. The Death card, for example, is not usually about the mortal concept of life ending. Rather, it is a card that asks us to give compassionate witness to the natural—and necessary—cycle of beginnings and endings. While it is intuitive to jump to familiar or traditional definitions of the titles of each of the Major Arcana, think of getting to know your deck as not only an opportunity to redefine words like "death," but an opportunity to rewrite your personal narrative and the perception of your life experiences.

THE ROOTS OF BEING AND THE OPENING TRUMP CARDS

"IF YOU WISH TO MAKE AN APPLE PIE FROM SCRATCH, YOU MUST FIRST INVENT THE UNIVERSE."

—CARL SAGAN (1934–1996),
scientist, visionary, humanitarian

We begin our hero's journey with the first card in the deck, the Fool. Interestingly, the beginning of the astrological calendar aligns with April Fool's Day in Europe and North America. This is the heart of fiery Aries season and the beginning of spring. This part of our journey's cycle symbolizes fresh starts, life, divinity, and childlike energy. In other words: We begin at the beginning.

The initiation of human life itself is almost too easy, even foolish; life is created from the playful, animalistic act of sex, only to be followed by the all-too-sobering romp through life wherein we are met with challenge after challenge, pain after pain, and endless suffering all in the pursuit of slowly gathering wisdom. In many ways, we start our journey through the tarot by rebirthing ourselves. We begin learning by first unlearning compulsory concepts of self and reimagining our own life paths. We are truly new humans each day. We are called to play with fire just as our ancestors did, test boundaries like the spirited toddlers we once were, and leap into life's great adventure with the reckless abandon and curiosity of the Fool.

"ALL GREAT DEEDS AND ALL GREAT THOUGHTS HAVE A RIDICULOUS BEGINNING. GREAT WORKS ARE OFTEN BORN ON A STREET CORNER OR IN A RESTAURANT'S REVOLVING DOOR."

—ALBERT CAMUS (1913–1960),
philosopher, journalist, Nobel Prize winner

These three trump cards—the Fool, Magician, and High Priestess—initiate us into the tarot, symbolizing the roots of our very existence. They are the sparks that fuel our pursuits of living meaningful lives. The Fool embodies bright, passionate energy, expression, freedom, and the cultivation of dreams and ambitions. The Magician has learned to channel these instincts into action using the tools they've gathered, much like we do in adolescence as we prepare to enter the world of adulthood. The High Priestess has lived enough life to see the path ahead as well as the underpinnings of what has been, what is, and what is yet to come.

While the Fool's power lies in leaping bravely ahead, the Magician knows how to balance compulsion and composition, and the High Priestess intuitively intertwines all the passion and intellect of the first two cards. We can also view the Fool as life (pure potential), the Magician as death (the mortal, unchangeable nature of life), and the High Priestess as rebirth (the knowledge that death is not an ending, but a mere step along the path). This cycle is a theme throughout the tarot, and you'll see it mentioned many times in this book and others.

"YOUR VISIONS WILL BECOME CLEAR ONLY WHEN YOU CAN LOOK INTO YOUR OWN HEART. WHO LOOKS OUTSIDE, DREAMS; WHO LOOKS INSIDE, AWAKES."

—CARL JUNG (1875–1961),
psychiatrist, world traveler, founder of analytical psychology

Some of us find ourselves residing in the territory of the opening trump cards quite often whether we choose our paths or find ourselves cast into them. For example, both of us were diagnosed as Autistic in our thirties. We each live with ADHD, and we each discovered our Queer identities through challenging journeys. We know rebirth quite well. In fact, we both embody the Fool in our rawest and most honest natures, the Magician in our creative bursts of otherworldly manifestation, and the High Priestess when we turn inward, swimming in the mysterious waters of the mind.

We begin here in earnest, in a raw and real state, moving through the first three steps of our hero's journey. We open our minds and hearts to new possibilities. Remember this: Denying your inner fire only allows it to wreak destruction.

May the path ahead blaze bright.

THE FOOL

The Fool is the card of the natural world, embodying a spirit of recklessness. The instinct to frolic into the wilds of life has taken over, and we find ourselves leaping across canyons into the unknown. While curiosity may have killed the cat, this card trusts that satisfaction with lessons learned along the way will bring the cat home.

So maybe it's a little reckless to run free, but . . . why not be a little reckless? Explore! Adventure! Express! Be the court jester who speaks brutal truth masked in humor. Now is a time for purity of thought and playfulness. Trust the raw impulses within you, no matter the result. It's time to jump.

REVERSED: Call yourself out when you are not trusting your instincts. What is holding you back from fully diving in? The reversed Fool shows up to give us a reality-checking slap in the face. Get back on the roller coaster of life, take that risk you've been avoiding, and don't worry about perfect planning. Be a fool and it might pay off in ways you'd never even imagined.

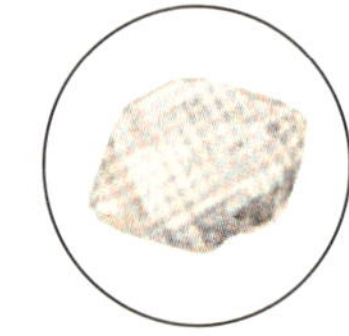

GEM

Clear quartz

PURE ENERGY, POWER, LIMITLESSNESS

Consider this stone a clean slate with which to work your magic.

SONG

"Dog Days Are Over"

FLORENCE + THE MACHINE

SCENT

FRESHLY CUT GRASS AND NEW BOOKS

NUMEROLOGY

0

INFINITY, WHOLENESS, LIMITLESS POTENTIAL, MYSTERY

The beginning of everything, and all that is to come.

The beginning is an awfully good place to start. Reflect below in whatever way you like—writing, doodling, scribbling—or take your responses off the page and into a journal, to a piano, or by using dance or movement of some kind.

WHAT DO YOU ASSOCIATE WITH . . .

. . . NEW BEGINNINGS?

. . . ADVENTURE?

. . . BRAVERY?

. . . NAIVETE?

. . . YOUTH?

THE MAGICIAN

The Magician is a master of the four suits—Wands, Cups, Swords, and Pentacles—and all four elements—fire, earth, air, and water. The wisdom of the Magician may seem like quite a jump from the youthful naivete of the Fool, but the Magician can represent the adolescent self, one who is excited to have gained access to the tools at their disposal. They look at the physical, creative, and spiritual tools at hand and know that results can be achieved if only they put in the work.

Channel your inner artist. Look around and within you to get a new perspective on the tools you have access to but have yet to master. The Magician calls us to create space for inspiration, to release what remains dormant.

REVERSED: Are you ignoring the resources you have? There may be something you're being (perhaps willfully) ignorant to. Time to get some clarity. Keep in mind, the Magician holds magnificent power to illuminate or deceive. Use your creativity to harness your power for good, to gain a clearer perception of how you may be living in delusion.

GEM

Hematite

CONFIDENCE, WILLPOWER, RESOURCEFULNESS

Use this supportive stone to boost confidence and manifest silver linings in the clouds surrounding you.

SONG

"Power"

LITTLE MIX

SCENT

NAG CHAMPA INCENSE

NUMEROLOGY

1

THE SUN, INITIATION, WILLPOWER

A direct, intense energy that is all about positivity and adventure.

BALANCING ELEMENTS

To wield magic is to perform a balancing act. The tarot helps us consider the importance and power of many facets of our lives; from the physical earth we stand on to the ways we treat our bodies. In the boxes below, write out some ways to access each tarot suit and your*self* to truly harness the power of the Magician.

SPIRIT | higher self, universe

BODY | life, health

SWORDS | air, thought

WANDS | fire, power

PENTACLES | earth, abundance

CUPS | water, emotions

THE HIGH PRIESTESS

She is the maiden, mother, and crone combined. The High Priestess knows that her place in the universe is one of unique divinity. When she shows up, she's telling you to pay attention to your subconscious—what can you see in the light of the moon? What secrets do you hold inside? How holy are the waters of your wisdom?

Spend time basking in your unique knowledge and experience. Use this magic by connecting with your community, perhaps as a peer mentor, poet, or even some kind of modern-day village witch.

REVERSED: You may be ignoring the reality of what's happening and your own gut instincts. Think back to a recent moment of tension: Consider what the root emotion was and what emotion may have bubbled up to hide the heart of the matter. Listen to the whispers of your inner self as they guide you toward clarity.

GEM

Labradorite

PSYCHIC PROTECTION, INTUITION, SAFETY

This gem protects the wearer from internal and external negativity.

SONG

"Gold Dust Woman"

FLEETWOOD MAC

SCENT

JASMINE

NUMEROLOGY

2

BALANCE AND UNITY

An alignment with the heavens and the Earth.

A cycle is anything that seems to follow a pattern that repeats. While many associate the word "cycle" with menstruation or moon phases, every human being regularly goes through their own cycles. Use this tracker to get in touch with your natural rhythm for the next thirty days and see what you discover.

TIP: Create a legend so tracking is easy, and keep this book by your bed or coffee cup, so it becomes part of your routine.

MOOD + BODY: + OVERALL:	MOOD + BODY: + OVERALL:	MOOD + BODY: + OVERALL:	MOOD + BODY: + OVERALL:	MOOD + BODY: + OVERALL:	MOOD + BODY: + OVERALL:
MOOD + BODY: + OVERALL:	MOOD + BODY: + OVERALL:	MOOD + BODY: + OVERALL:	MOOD + BODY: + OVERALL:	MOOD + BODY: + OVERALL:	MOOD + BODY: + OVERALL:
MOOD + BODY: + OVERALL:	MOOD + BODY: + OVERALL:	MOOD + BODY: + OVERALL:	MOOD + BODY: + OVERALL:	MOOD + BODY: + OVERALL:	MOOD + BODY: + OVERALL:
MOOD + BODY: + OVERALL:	MOOD + BODY: + OVERALL:	MOOD + BODY: + OVERALL:	MOOD + BODY: + OVERALL:	MOOD + BODY: + OVERALL:	MOOD + BODY: + OVERALL:
MOOD + BODY: + OVERALL:	MOOD + BODY: + OVERALL:	MOOD + BODY: + OVERALL:	MOOD + BODY: + OVERALL:	MOOD + BODY: + OVERALL:	MOOD + BODY: + OVERALL:
MOOD + BODY: + OVERALL:	DON'T WORRY IF YOU MISS A DAY! That's part of your cycle too. Just fill in "forgot" or an X and see what pattern might emerge from this awareness.				

THE PURSUIT OF EXTERNAL EXPERIENCE AND WORLDLY KNOWLEDGE

When we're young, the exploration of self is full of wonder and magic. As we turn our attention outward, influenced by our guardians and educators (the earliest and most influential external forces that shape who we become), we encounter nature, society, and organized religion and government.

The Empress, Emperor, and Hierophant embody these external influences and act as the holy trinity of the tarot. The mother and father figures cultivate the rules, regulations, and decrees of the Hierophant, the earthly leader who connects us to mystical, otherworldly wisdom. The Lovers and the Chariot take what is learned from the trinity and turn to action. The Lovers card encourages exploration of oneself within relationships, and the Chariot encourages the expression of the self to an almost glorified degree.

Mother Nature, embodied by the Empress, holds powerful feminine energy (see "Queering the Concept of 'Masculine' and 'Feminine,'" page 10). She is the root of creation itself, fueled by sensuality and indulgence. She encourages us to lean into impulses and connect with our bodies, leading with empathy and joy. The Emperor embodies all that is opposite yet harmonic with the Empress. The Emperor exists in an intellectual realm and takes on masculine qualities of strategy, leadership, and authority. He and the Empress remain grounded, representing the earthbound power of society.

The Hierophant (sometimes called the Pope, Popess, or High Priest) is a symbol of the structures that influence a person's intellect. This archetype asks us to receive education with an open mind and discern whether to integrate, adapt, or reject that information. It would be shortsighted to try to understand the wisdom of the Hierophant without first considering our own intuitive wisdom (represented by the Empress) and society's influence (the Emperor). The trinity works best in harmony—no one source of knowledge is "right," but all help to balance and inform one another.

The Lovers card represents duality and the relationship we, as individuals, have with the Other. The Other may be a person, thought, or feeling within ourselves that contradicts, influences, or challenges what already exists. While lovers can represent unity, there is a natural push and pull of opposing forces. Like sex itself, the tension and excitement found in the Lovers paves a path to a climactic tipping point.

Many hero's stories climax with a triumphant champion parading through the streets in his chariot. The Chariot symbolizes just that, a person experiencing their first big win. Influenced by the Lovers, it can mean the raw thrill of burgeoning sexuality. Or the win can speak to independence, the first great point of separation from the Empress, Emperor, and Hierophant. No matter the situation, the Chariot is a celebration.

As you work with these cards, reflect on your teen years: the aches, pains, and first awkward challenges of growing up. The path to higher knowledge requires steps through each of these archetypes. Play, explore, and take it all in with wide-open eyes. Test, integrate, reject, and triumph. It's essential to your growth, no matter your age. We are perpetually in motion and destined to meet each of these cards many times over in our cycles through life.

"BE BRAVE. TAKE RISKS.
NOTHING CAN SUBSTITUTE EXPERIENCE."

—PAULO COELHO (1947–),
multidisciplinary artist, author, world traveler

THE EMPRESS

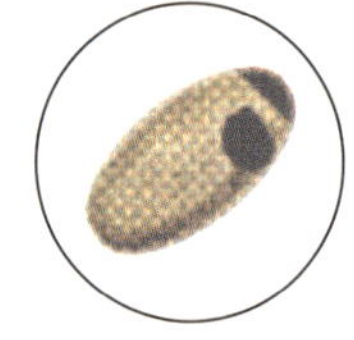

The Empress knows how to *feel.* Rather than being concerned with how we "should" feel, we must listen to what our bodies demand, pairing emotional and physical intuition. Are you listening to what your vessel needs? Give yourself compassion: Feeling is often excruciating. Luxuriate in your vulnerability.

Consider how to increase awareness of your physical needs and desires. How might you release the "shoulds" society has encouraged you to take on? Because the thing is, you were once a wild thing. You have been domesticated. It is time to become feral and reunite with your senses. Even through tears.

REVERSED: Are you living by rules you never agreed to? Ask yourself: *Did I even sign up to play this game?* If you got yourself into a mess, that is okay. Consider how to move forward and create change. There is some repression at play, but your feelings are going to demand to be felt until you give in, so listen up. Reconnect to nature's beautiful wildness and get your hands dirty, connect to your roots.

GEM

Shiva lingam

SENSUALITY, SOFTNESS, HONESTY

This stone represents the Hindu god Shiva, the transformer and destroyer of illusions, the ultimate creator.

SONG

"I AM WOMAN"

EMMY MELI

SCENT

ROSES IN FULL BLOOM

NUMEROLOGY

3

DELICIOUS, RADICAL, DIVINE

This is Venus's number, representing love and sensuality.

SENSUAL ACTIVATION

Use this ritual to tap into your most sensual self. List a few sweet associations you have with each of the senses. Choose one item from each list and create a sensuality ritual. For example, try speaking or writing down an intention. Light a candle for the duration of the ritual. At the end, speak or write your gratitude for what you experienced and blow out the candle.

SMELL | amber, bonfire, the ocean

TOUCH | my dog's fur, velvet, a warm bath

TASTE | sour candy, hot coffee, seltzer bubbles

SOUND | birds in the morning, my favorite song, my friends' laughter

SIGHT | sunset, a clean bathroom, Matisse paintings

THE EMPEROR

The Daddy of the tarot, the Emperor represents discipline and unyielding power. This can, in the best of situations, look like ruling with full confidence and wisdom. In the worst cases, it can look like oligarchy and fascism. The trick to being a wise Emperor is to remember the cards that came before—the beautiful young Fool, the resourceful Magician, the mysterious High Priestess, the nurturing Empress. As our lives progress, we must integrate all iterations of ourselves rather than leave them behind. The pieces work together to create a more realized self, and the Emperor embodies this holistic, stable strength.

REVERSED: The time to get off the high horse has come. The Emperor may be a ruler, but they are still just a human being. Ego trips often look like narcissism but may actually be a result of insecure self-hatred. Ask yourself why being "better" or "worse" than others gives you a sense of self. When you strip away the comparisons, what are you left with? That's where your power lies.

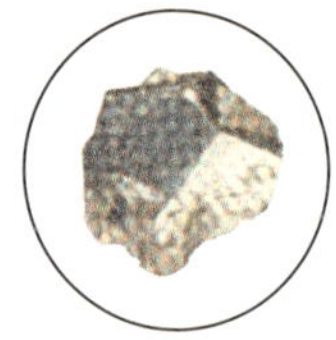

GEM

Pyrite

WEALTH, ABUNDANCE, PROTECTION

Known for providing luck, pyrite also represents the ideal of masculine energy—passion, energy, and a sense of safety.

SONG

"Masculinity"

SAMORA PINDERHUGHES (FEATURING IMMANUEL WILKINS)

SCENT

LEATHER AND EXPENSIVE WHISKEY

NUMEROLOGY

4

STABILITY, COURAGE, FORTITUDE

This strong number presents itself with confidence and logic.

ENERGETIC INVESTING

The Emperor always keeps their checkbook balanced. Consider the energetic input and output of your daily life—your earnings, investments, deposits, and withdrawals—using spoon theory, a metaphor that illustrates the unique "cost" of energy for an individual to perform everyday tasks.

Coined by the writer Christine Miserandino, "spoon theory" offers the visual of a handful of spoons that represent the finite amount of daily energy a person has. Some people wake up with more "spoons" than others. Some tasks may require more "spoons" for one person than they would another, due to chronic illness, disability, trauma, or income, among other reasons.

Assess your own "spoons" and then consider any imbalances. How can you find balance?

THE THINGS THAT ADD TO MY ENERGY (e.g., rest, socializing with a specific person, Sudoku):

THE THINGS THAT COST ME ENERGY (e.g., work, that one rude cousin, chronic illness):

SHORT-TERM INVESTMENTS (e.g., saving for travel, working late on passion projects):

LONG-TERM INVESTMENTS (e.g., therapy, saving for retirement):

THE HIEROPHANT

Mentorship, guidance, and knowledge gained are the key elements of the Hierophant. It's time to seek out new or deeper teachings. Whether you are in pursuit of practical or spiritual knowledge, your resource for wisdom is just around the corner. Be wary of attaching too heavily to charismatic leaders. Teachers are here to give you resources for your own learning. Avoid houses of learning that preach a singular narrative of one path or one truth.

So many spiritual, emotional, physical, and cerebral spaces of education intersect. Observing the threads of wisdom woven through the ages will help you gain deeper knowledge. No single path can complete you. *You* complete you. And so, seek guidance and variety in the ways you acquire information.

REVERSED: Rejecting tradition or expectation purely because it's expected isn't necessarily the right move. Now is the moment to examine the motivation behind certain choices—whether they're ours or someone else's—and be aware:

You can only change yourself and your actions. Have you become entangled in a corrupt situation? Use logic to see through the fog of uncertainty.

GEM

Nuummite

SPIRITUALITY, WISDOM, CLEANSING

An aid for an enhanced spiritual life, especially for those traveling the path of overcoming deep wounds from their past.

SONG

"The Knowledge"

JANET JACKSON

SCENT

FRANKINCENSE AND MYRRH

NUMEROLOGY

5

CURIOSITY, ADAPTABILITY, ENERGY

5 is inherently chaotic; this creative intensity can be used for good.

Think of an inspirational person you look up to but do not know. It could be someone brave who forges new paths forward toward knowledge like Malala Yousafzai, someone who encompasses creativity at any cost like Marina Abramović, or someone who can hold many truths at once like Alok Vaid Menon.

MY IMAGINED MENTOR IS . . .

Take a deep breath and close your eyes. Imagine living your mentor's life—immerse yourself. Then open your eyes and respond as if your mentor were giving advice.

WHAT SHOULD I DO WHEN I'M AFRAID OF FAILING?

HOW DO I OVERCOME RESISTANCE TO DOING WHAT IS IN MY BEST INTEREST?

THE BEST ADVICE I HAVE FOR A LIFE WELL-LIVED IS . . .

THE LOVERS

We see this card and think of romance, new-relationship energy, and yummy, sexy feelings. It's important, however, to remember that the Lovers speaks most strongly to our sense of self-love. Tarot is a mirror that reflects our inner workings and the Lovers shows us what's inside our hearts.

For any union to succeed and bear fruit, everyone involved must accept and embrace the multiplicity of selves within. To truly cultivate romance and love with another, romance *yourself*. You are, first and foremost, your own deity, life partner, and facilitator of power and beauty. The Lovers prompts you to explore the sensuality of the self. Follow the path that leads deepest within, toward wholeness and the fruitful destiny ahead.

REVERSED: Somewhere in your heart, there's a misalignment of values. You're finding yourself feeling unsatisfied and unsure, whether it's in a relationship with someone else or in the relationship to self. Take a moment to analyze the internal conflict. You are being prompted to realign with your core truths.

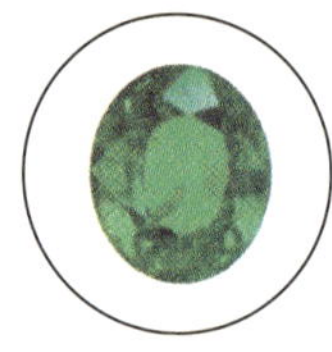

GEM

Emerald

PATIENCE, COMPASSION, GROWTH

When you need a serious dose of luxurious adoration, emerald radiates love, beauty, and sex. Wear it over your heart.

SONG

"Soulmate"

LIZZO

SCENT

LAVENDER AND FRESH LINENS

NUMEROLOGY

6

COMPATIBILITY, LIFE PATH, ALIGNMENT

Think of 6 as the earthly mother Gaia, the giver of unconditional love, the hearth that warms your core.

THE SYMBOLISM OF NUDITY

When we find ourselves fearful of being naked in its many forms—whether it's nudity, vulnerability, or exposing truths—challenge that fear. When you risk revealing your naked and true self to yourself or someone else, allow the rush of nervous energy to be a form of arousal. Reward yourself with something that will drive a climax, be it sex, buying something you love, or eating something delicious. Train your senses to lust for naked truth that results in reward.

What does it look and feel like to be naked with yourself:

EMOTIONALLY? ______________________________

____

____

PHYSICALLY? ______________________________

____

____

SPIRITUALLY? ______________________________

____

____

What does it look and feel like to be naked with someone else:

EMOTIONALLY? ______________________________

____

____

PHYSICALLY? ______________________________

____

____

SPIRITUALLY? ______________________________

____

____

THE CHARIOT

Life is full of yeses and nos. We receive directives from others, but only we can decide whether to adhere to the answers we are given. Willpower and willfulness: Do you know the difference? The Chariot arises when we are being challenged to harness our own willpower and trust ourselves.

Your objectives have been set and your inner fire will ignite your heart's devotion. You will encounter bumps and divots along this journey, but trust that your heart's fire is strong enough to fuel you. Commit yourself to self-discipline and prepare strategically for the obstacles ahead. What are you willing to push your wheels through with brute force? What is not worth your energy? Know when to say no, the ultimate power move.

REVERSED: It's time for a U-turn. The reversed Chariot is an alert for the safety of mind, body, and soul. Use your willpower to pause and reassess your direction. No one outside of you will see this shift coming. Shock them with your strategic pivot.

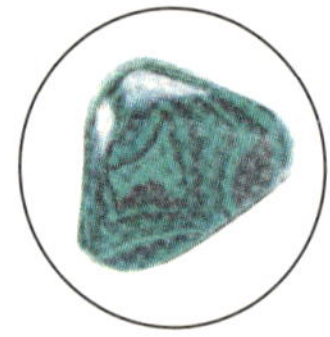

GEM

Malachite

PROTECTION, TRAVEL, LOGIC

Malachite's power aids in transformation, ensures safety, and encourages accountability.

SONG

"No Looking Back"

GENESIS OWUSU

SCENT

AIR CONDITIONING AND COCONUT OIL

NUMEROLOGY

7

PSYCHIC VISIONS, PROGRESS, INTERNAL JOURNEY

Under Neptune's influence, those who attach to the number 7 are immersed in fantasy, for better or worse.

The Chariot calls you to be bold, to push ahead with a wild fantasy. Let's explore audacious ideas. Let your mind go wild and list five dreams that feel almost ridiculous, fanciful, thrilling—the kind that if they came true would blow your mind!

1. ______

2. ______

3. ______

4. ______

5. ______

NAME A TIME IN THE PAST WHEN YOU PURSUED SOMETHING WITH RECKLESS ABANDON:

______

______

______

______

______

______

Take a risk this week, allowing fantasy to be a friend. Pursue one of your audacious goals every day this week, and whether it results in anything or not, explore your feelings after a week of trying. There is power in the pursuit of fantasy.

THE EXPLORATION OF OUR INNER SELVES

As we turn inward after enjoying the delicious, temporary high of the Chariot, we come to realize that success alone cannot sustain a soul. Once the craving for a taste of glory is satiated, what comes next?

Throughout history, we've held different names for the season of inward exploration. A critic may call this reckoning of self a midlife crisis, while spiritualists may call it Saturn's return. The sixteenth-century Catholic priest and mystic Saint John of the Cross called it "the dark night of the soul." This period is the voyage from Strength to the Hanged One, a path that leads to who we truly are and what we most need.

Stoic Strength is an embodiment of all opposing forces in the universe that truly balance one another. It is to our advantage to find peace in our contradictions and the gray in a world of black and white: between feminine and masculine, cerebral and emotional, extroversion and introversion, chaos and order. In Strength we sit comfortably unbiased, observing the true state of our inner and outer worlds with acceptance. This leads us into the Hermit, a symbol of sacred aloneness and introspection. In our younger years, we seek validation of self from others. But true maturity requires us to balance the external and internal.

The Hermit harkens back to free-thinkers of ancient times who isolated to focus on inner mystical explanation. They were often seen as an oracle, a profoundly valuable community member. The modern Western world, which thrives on capitalism, often views those who think outside the box as disordered or dysfunctional. In societies truly rooted in community, however, these seers are respected.

The Wheel of Fortune is a shocking tumble, spinning us around to challenge previous viewpoints and prepare for future opportunities. When we once felt on top of the world, riding in the Chariot and feeling in control of our path, the Wheel of Fortune speaks to the randomness and mystery of fate itself. It tells us to welcome the chaos inherent to life. There's a saying that luck is when preparation and opportunity meet—that's the Wheel of Fortune. Expect the unexpected.

Justice is the scale that balances past and present, the internal and external, the rational and intuitive. This card is the heart and soul of the question "Is this it?" It is a pausing point of reassessment. Justice encourages a fine-tuning, an awareness of the greater purpose our soul aches to fulfill. Once we embrace this gray area, we are elevated to the Hanged One, an enlightened being who hovers above the madness of the world in stillness.

Many occultists throughout history have been influenced by the practice of yoga, seeking greater awareness by literally standing on their heads. In this reversal of posture, we can see a physical example of the conceptual reversal of one's attitude in response to spiritual awakening. We see this in the Hanged One. This card calls for yet another change in perspective, this time so that we are not swallowed up by the world at large and are peaceful in our stillness.

"MINDFUL AWARENESS CAN BRING INTO CONSCIOUSNESS THOSE HIDDEN, PAST-BASED PERSPECTIVES SO THAT THEY NO LONGER FRAME OUR WORLDVIEW. 'CHOICE BEGINS THE MOMENT YOU DISIDENTIFY FROM THE MIND AND ITS CONDITIONED PATTERNS, THE MOMENT YOU BECOME PRESENT . . . UNTIL YOU REACH THAT POINT, YOU ARE UNCONSCIOUS.' . . . IN PRESENT AWARENESS WE ARE LIBERATED FROM THE PAST."

— **GABOR MATÉ (1944–),**
author & physician

STRENGTH

We often assume strength is a solitary, stoic experience—that a person must stand confidently alone to embody such power. In truth, compassion and humility are key to building strength that sustains us. Where the Chariot speaks to will and strategic power, Strength speaks to a softer inner knowing.

Your inner strength leads others to see you as a source of inspiration. Your influence is subtle yet permeating. The more you show up with gentleness, forgiveness, and love, the more you will see your work and identity become integral to others'. Strength asks you to practice guiding others slowly, while you apply the same pace to your life and work. There is no rush.

REVERSED: Time for a check-in. Are you feeling overly confident? Or perhaps a heavy dose of self-doubt? Any explosive thoughts or feelings? Pause. Think about what you have said to yourself this week. Write down some examples to see the proof that you need time to restore your energy levels. Consider where you draw your energy and confidence from.

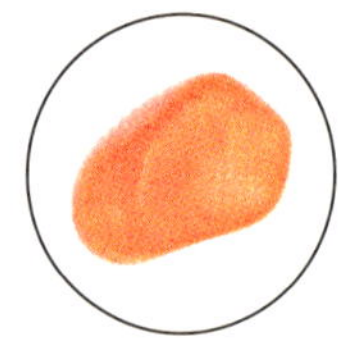

GEM

Carnelian

CONFIDENCE, GROUNDING, CREATIVITY

For those in need of a boost of courage; carry it as you move past trauma, heal from abuse, and find yourself.

SONG

"Tightrope"

JANELLE MONÁE (FEATURING BIG BOI)

SCENT

A HOME-COOKED MEAL

NUMEROLOGY

8

BALANCE, INSPIRATION, SUCCESS

A symbol of infinity, an ever-churning cycle of patterns, evolution, and momentum.

CHALLENGE YOUR STRENGTH

Each day this week, use the prompts below to build holistic personal strength. If you find yourself feeling a boost of confidence, positivity, happiness, and healthy pride due to your efforts this week, keep the challenge going next week!

- ○ **MENTAL:** Complete a Sudoku or crossword puzzle, teach yourself a few words from a different language, or play a mental game on an app.
- ○ **EMOTIONAL:** Express gratitude for someone in your life, practice self-control when you feel impulsive, journal about your emotional state, or ask for help when you need it.
- ○ **PHYSICAL:** Try a new workout, go for a walk in a new space, do some deep stretching, hold a plank position for as long as you can, or find a local spot to go swimming.
- ○ **RELATIONSHIP:** Show affection for someone you love, seek out a new friendship, make someone you love a meal or baked good, or, when someone vents to you next, ask, "Would you like me to just listen or offer advice?"
- ○ **FINANCIAL:** Start a savings account for something you're dreaming of, take a few unused items to a consignment store to sell, or contribute five dollars to a savings account.
- ○ **HEALTH:** Make a doctor's appointment you've been avoiding, make a healthy and delicious meal, get eight hours of sleep, or avoid alcohol for a week.
- ○ **CREATIVE:** Draw something funny, write a poem, build something, sing a song, make an inspiration board, or paint an object in your home a new color.

THE HERMIT

It's okay to retreat. Sometimes life can leave us feeling the need for a little respite from the day-to-day, even from our beloveds. Needing alone time and isolation is natural, and giving yourself the time to indulge in healing is a major gift. You may feel restless taking time off, and if so, consider this: If you're used to going too hard for too long, it *will* feel unusual to slow down.

Give yourself permission to ignore outside noise and zone in on your own needs. Your inner world is your fuel. Fill your own cup so that when you reemerge, you can pour into others'. In this moment, you are the magical chrysalis that will transform into a butterfly with time.

REVERSED: You may be avoiding something important. Are you isolating to the point of sabotaging relationships, work, or other parts of your life? Be realistic: Do you really need this separation or are you just ignoring reality? Do some digging and see if something is holding you back. Remember that starting is always the hardest part.

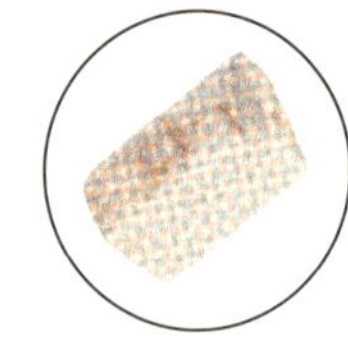

GEM

Selenite

PEACE, SERENITY, HEALING

This classic crystal for cleansing the energy in any room is ultimate harmony in a sparkly little package.

SONG

"You Can Never Hold Back Spring"

TOM WAITS

SCENT

EARL GREY TEA AND A ROARING FIREPLACE

NUMEROLOGY

9

REFLECTION, INDIVIDUALITY, APPROACHING COMPLETION

We are nearing the end of a journey—and to achieve the best outcome, we must reflect on what's happened up until this point.

A ONE-DAY HERMITAGE

For many of us, taking time away feels impossible. That is where the *self-date* comes in. Connect with the spirit of the Hermit by planning your perfect day flying solo. Consider what you would plan for a new crush, what you'd wear, how you would treat them, and what activities you would create to woo them. Or think about what would be thrilling (even if that also means a little intimidating) to do on this day!

MY PERFECT MORNING CONSISTS OF ______________________________

____

How would you begin the perfect day? What's your favorite breakfast? What time is your ideal to wake up?

A PLACE I'D LOVE TO GO BY MYSELF IS ______________________________

____

Fiji and Italy might sound exciting, but it's probably a challenge to get there this weekend. Where can you go for this hermitage, here and now?

CREATIVE IDEAS FOR HOW TO MAKE THIS HAPPEN INCLUDE ______________

____

____

____

This might be childcare options, budgetary planning, researching local events, etc.

WHAT ARE SOME THINGS THAT YOU'D LOVE TO TRY DOING ALONE? __________

____

____

____

Going to a movie by yourself, eating lunch at a beautiful café and bringing your watercolors, or even something big like taking a trip might be just what you need.

THE WHEEL OF FORTUNE

Halfway through the hero's journey, one leg of the trip has come to an end and another has begun. You're right-side up then suddenly you're upside-down and uncertain. *Trust* is the name of this game.

Remember, there are stages of change. The first upheaval may feel like *the* big moment, but change is an evolution, not a singular event. One minute you're a caterpillar, crawling on leaves, embodying a grounded state of knowing. Then you're turning to goo inside a chrysalis. All you can do is *be*, reflect on what once was, and keep an open mind for what comes next. It's natural to worry. Trust nature as it helps you build yourself again, this time with more wisdom, radiance, and the capacity to truly lift off and fly.

REVERSED: Are you trying to manipulate outcomes beyond your control? Are you unwilling to accept what lies ahead? Trust the universe, regardless of how challenging that might be. It will work out, one way or another.

GEM

Aventurine

PERSEVERANCE, BALANCE, ANTI-INFLAMMATION

Aventurine is a stabilizing force during times of change, soothing physical stress and clearing blockages from your emotional center.

SONG

"Extraordinary Machine"

FIONA APPLE

SCENT

A WARM SPRING BREEZE THROUGH AN OPEN CAR WINDOW

NUMEROLOGY

10

COMPLETION, REINVENTION, AMPLIFICATION

Containing 1 and 0, 10 is a booming echo or a beginning, powerful and wise.

TRUSTING INTUITION

One of the most challenging parts of listening to our intuition is not knowing what intuition physiologically feels like. This practice is to help develop awareness of our inner knowing so we can trust our feelings, instincts, and perception.

1. Find a two-sided coin. You'll need to decide which side of the coin represents yes and which represents no.
2. Ask your coin a series of yes-or-no questions that you already know the answer to. For example, *Is my name xyz? Is today June 30? Was I born in the United States?* Flip the coin after each question and check the result.
3. With every answer, notice what you feel in your body and where. Notice the sensations and emotions that emerge with each yes and no.
4. Repeat this process multiple times until you know for sure what "correct" and "incorrect" answers feel like in your body.

Once you know what right and wrong *feel* like, listen to your body when you need reassurance. Journal about this process so you can reflect over time and stay mindful of your experience as it changes.

JUSTICE

Justice is the card of truth. Something needs adjustment. If that which has driven you lately doesn't feel restorative or authentic, prepare for accountability. If you're waiting for justice to be served, this is a sign that your challenges are concluding. It's also a reminder that in any battle, both parties' problems are valid *and* both must take accountability if resolution is the goal.

Do you trust your decisions? Are you willing to accept the consequences? Can you own your part and release it? Dig deep to find security in your choices. Are you being honest with yourself?

REVERSED: Your inner critic has been rampaging. What if you looked at your past with acceptance instead of regret? Painful and unpleasant as it may be, there is nothing you can do to change what's happened. In this moment, accept with forgiveness and compassion: *What is done is done and I'll make more informed decisions now.* With mistakes come the gifts of growth and wisdom.

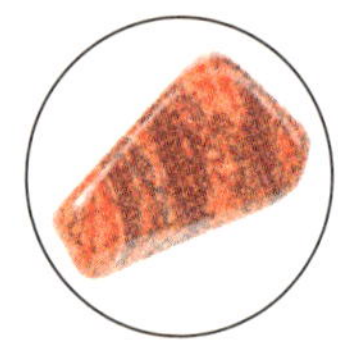

GEM

Jasper

EMOTION REGULATION, NURTURING, WHOLENESS

In times of duress, this gem supports the nervous system.

SONG

"We Shall Overcome"

LOUIS ARMSTRONG

SCENT

INKY DOCUMENTS AND INCENSE

NUMEROLOGY

11

DIVINITY, EQUALITY, CLARITY

A "master number" with an emphasis of the qualities of 1 via repetition, while also holding the qualities of 2 (1 + 1 = 2).

It can be challenging to know what's "right" and what's "wrong." The time-tested method of listing pros and cons works well, but most people don't know the original intention behind the practice. A pros-and-cons list is an exercise in balance. As you write the pros and cons of a situation, cross out list items that balance each other out. It's when we find higher-value items that don't cancel each other out that we get a clear picture of how to move forward.

Using two columns, list out your reasons to make a challenging decision and see what ends up weighing more.

PROS	CONS

TIP: When in doubt, turn to a trusted friend and show them the list, or at the very least, tell them your sticking points. What's keeping you from being able to choose?

THE HANGED ONE

You've come a long way and now strategy needs to shift. Take a moment to look out from your new vantage point. What's revealing itself to you? Consider this, and then flip the world upside down to examine everything with fresh eyes.

While you might feel stuck, don't fight it. Don't forget your wisdom . . . and that the *point* is to finally release control. Picture yourself hanging upside down from a tree like a child, swinging from strong legs. The space you're in isn't one to fear—revel in it. Allow the world to pass you by as you look on from a place of power. You're safe here.

REVERSED: In what way are you clinging to control? When our grip is stubborn, we are destined for a breaking point. Let go before the universe builds further tension and drops you. You and only you have the capacity to release and rest. Discover the freedom in sitting back and watching what happens.

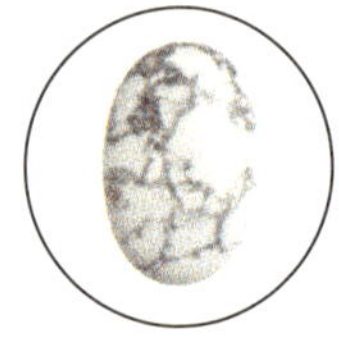

GEM

Howlite

PATIENCE, PERSPECTIVE, MINDFULNESS

Howlite teaches the value of pausing. Hold it during transformation.

SONG

"Let Go"

FROU FROU

SCENT

CHERRY BLOSSOMS AND SELTZER FIZZ

NUMEROLOGY

12

EVOLUTION, CYCLES, PROCESS

Twelve is an amplified 3 (1 + 2 = 3) and relates to divine order and the cycle of all things.

WALL INVERSION

One of the easiest ways to reset your nervous system is to do any form of physical inversion. This forces the brain to recognize where it is in space, which can calm us in moments of panic, fight-or-flight, or other dysregulation.

To achieve the soothing effects of inversion, you can do a headstand, handstand, use an inversion table, or simply lie on your back and prop your legs up straight against a wall. The goal is to get your ankles as high above your head as possible.

Take a deep breath and let it out slowly, focusing on the sensations in your body from head to toe. Place a hand on your chest and continue to feel the rise and fall of each breath.

From this perspective and place of grounding, how does your current situation appear? Do you notice any thoughts popping up? Any sensations in your body? Keep breathing and witness yourself. Allow the thoughts to come, and then go.

THE EPIC QUEST TO ENLIGHTENMENT

The Death card is not something to fear; it is a breakthrough, an entry into deeper awareness, an initiation. It speaks to natural transformation and demands we accept it as an essential rite of passage.

After a traumatic experience like Death, Temperance is our first new friend, holding gently—but firmly—the many facets of our past and present selves. It speaks the language of the middle path, approaching all situations with understanding of all perspectives. Often, the right thing to do when faced with a challenge is nothing at all. Temperance urges us to avoid extremes and to find value in process. With this awareness, we can face the metaphorical demons ahead.

"The narrative of being a fully realized, enlightened being is a myth," the Devil whispers, attempting to keep us shackled to shame and self-hatred. We can't ignore our shadows, starving them of the love they need to heal. We must do this work compassionately. If we deny our shadow selves safe refuge and simultaneous freedom, the energy of entrapment builds. That's when we see the flash of lightning crack through the Tower.

The Tower's meaning depends on the reader's relationship with the Devil. When we accept that the Devil is cunning—a youthful trickster aspect of the self, always vying for attention—the upheaval of the Tower symbolizes the shattering of a false mirror. If we deny the power of the Devil, repression expands, becoming a supercharged target for the chaotic lightning that demolishes the Tower. If the Tower shows up in your readings, resistance is futile; it's coming whether you shake your fist to the sky or not.

But storms do pass. The Tower crumbled down to just the arch of a doorway, and in the Star, we step forward, finding refuge in the in-between. It tells us to be still and welcome the quiet revelations of the subconscious. In this card, we drink from the restorative waters of the divine and pour back into our earthly life. The Moon card facilitates a union between our perception and reality, washing us in contemplative light. In many ways, the Moon is the card of the imagination, gathering inspiration and helping us translate our desires and dreams into reality. Enjoy your time dreaming, but remember, we must wake with the rising of the Sun.

Finally, after journeying through the powerful latter half of the Major Arcana, we remember the vibrancy we had at the beginning of this journey. The Sun gives us the energy necessary to take action, embodying a sacred lucidity that allows us to greet Judgment with an open mind. Judgment dictates that we live a more meaningful life in unabashed, honest awareness. There's freedom from illusion, projection, and assumption within this place of knowing. It leaves no room for denial, only total acceptance that magic lives within all beings and even the most mundane objects.

We've now connected the heart, mind, body, and soul, drawing power from all elements. True wholeness is the essence of the World card. Here, we accept all that is within and outside of us as a community that works together. In many ways we are complete, yet . . . just around the corner comes the Fool once again.

On our next journey, we'll carry these lessons with us. For a moment, bask in this conclusion while also understanding that this too shall pass. Here, we end and begin again.

DEATH

Something deep inside you has begun to shift. You are clearer about who you are and it's time to say goodbye to something that once defined you. It could be an interest, a job, a relationship, or a facet of your persona. Knowing that you are becoming something—someone—else can feel like a loss. But the truth is, in releasing this thing that has found its end, you are creating an opening for new life.

Death is essential to growth. Think of the incredible nutrients found in compost. The ends of past lives can create a rich bed of earth to nurture roots for new life. The Death card may greet you in a moment of darkness, but remember you have the power to create an illuminated path forward toward an abundant future. Greet Death with a warm embrace and it will guide you to where you are meant to grow and thrive.

REVERSED: Are you resisting what you know needs to shift? Fear of the unknown and avoidance make change hard, but by avoiding change, you are prolonging your discomfort. Assess what you are clinging to. In release, you will find relief.

GEM

Aragonite

TRUTH, REALITY, CLARIFICATION

Keep it close when you feel the need to retreat into meditation on your path to deeper clarity and tolerance.

SONG

"Ascension"

MOSES SUMNEY

SCENT

WHITE LILIES

NUMEROLOGY

13

FORTUNE, STABILITY, HOLISTIC WELL-BEING

Some cultures view 13 as an unlucky number, but others see it as one of fortune. Simplify it to 4 (1 + 3 = 4) to remember that this is a number representing stability.

COMPASSIONATE BANISHMENT

When we honor the life of someone, we are providing closure for ourselves and the spirit in question. For the spirit, we do not know what comes next, but wakes and funerals are a way to send our beloveds off with support, love, and honor for the next phase of existence. For us, the part that comes after a loved one dies is integral to our story; by allowing ourselves to be fully present, we honor the presence that person had in our life. We make space for grief to take hold and change us as we adapt.

For this ritual, we are honoring the part of yourself that has come to an end. Consider it a wake for the living soul.

1. **GET DRESSED IN REGALIA.** Whether opulence or minimalism makes you feel more gravity, go for it.
2. **SET THE SCENE.** Is your wake in a sunny park? At a body of water? Are there flowers or lit candles? Wherever you feel you are meant to initiate this release, go to that place to honor the pieces of yourself that have fallen away.
3. **WRITE YOUR EULOGY.** Speak words of love for the part of yourself that's passed. Tell stories to yourself about the best and worst moments. Honor that process. You can physically write this down or speak it aloud. Create the spell of storytelling and wish your spirit well—both the part that has left and the part that remains.

Allow this ritual to close the door on the pieces of you which no longer make sense to carry forward. Walk through this threshold with love and sovereignty. If you struggle with this, sit with the Fool card and allow its young wisdom to flood your senses with adventure and excitement. Continue forward. Temperance awaits!

TEMPERANCE

Temperance takes trust and deep balance. In stressful moments we all doubt our purpose, but in pausing we're allowed observation. Look at the variety of tools that hang in your tool belt, the collected diverse experiences that inform the person you are. Perhaps you can see where your own past inclinations, habits, and conditioned responses may have sabotaged a more favorable possibility. But this doesn't mean there are regrets so much as there's new awareness. Instead of rushing to "fix" imperfections, take a moment to consider your next move; there's no sense of urgency here.

It is with these many observations, understandings, and earned skills that we navigate our inner and outer worlds. If there was ever a time to trust in your ability to forge stability, it is now. Trust in this enlightened state of self-awareness and peace.

REVERSED: You've recently indulged to the point of imbalance, perhaps from a place of discontent or anxiety. Now that it's come to the surface, trust your ability to make necessary adjustments to your habits which will, in turn, ease your mental state—and life—back into flow.

GEM

Copper
ALCHEMY, TRANSFORMATION, RENEWAL

Copper creates channels through conflict and stagnancy.

SONG

"Los Ageless"
ST. VINCENT

SCENT

BONFIRE

NUMEROLOGY

14
CHAOS, REDISTRIBUTION, ALIGNMENT

There are five (1 + 4 = 5) equal aspects to the pentacle—earth, air, water, fire, spirit. Make sure to use your energy equally.

A BASE OF BALANCE

In ancient Greece, the pentacle was regarded as a symbol of health and knowledge in its perfection. It's soothing to our eyes and creates a sense of balance within our minds because of its aesthetic perfection. In the pentacle below, observe the five cornerstones of a whole and healthy life.

Choose one suggestion from each pentacle point to focus on pursuing this week as a way to holistically care for your needs.

THE DEVIL

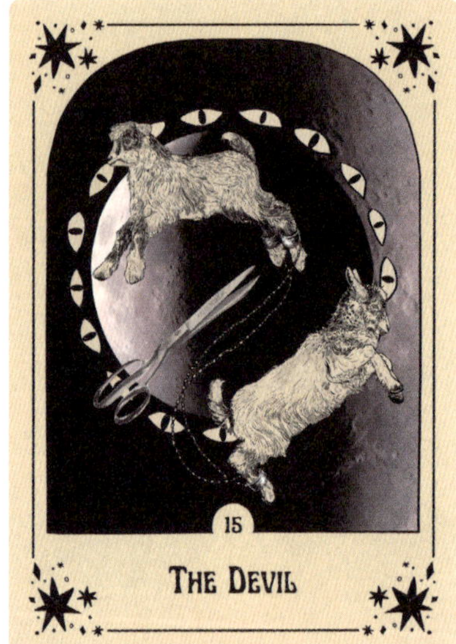

The Devil is our innermost critic, the part of ourselves that has been shaped by shame and guilt. It holds us hostage, yanking the chain of confinement whenever we venture too far from our trauma. Do not react in anger and instead, consider "the devil" for what it is: a reflection of ourselves.

Reframe your idea of your inner critic as your inner child. It is the part of us longing for validation and softness, but also needing parenting. When these hurt parts of ourselves demand our attention, how must we approach them? Explore boundaries with your most tender, traumatized selves while also honoring their struggle. Acceptance is your path to finally feeling free.

REVERSED: You've overcome much in this life. Use the lessons you've learned along the way to aid in your current situation. Feeling triggered by old memories? Consider how you reacted to past obstacles so that you may move through your current challenges with grace.

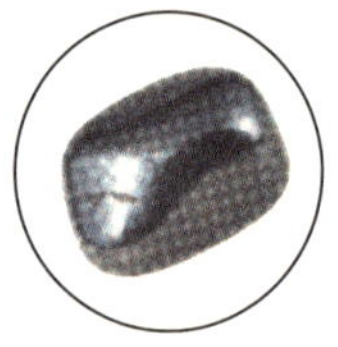

GEM

Black onyx
SELF-CONTROL, PROTECTION, DISCIPLINE

Hold this stone close when sadness, grief, and misfortune have clouded your vision.

SONG

"Muddy Waters"
LP

SCENT

YOUR ONE TRUE VICE

NUMEROLOGY

15
MIND, BODY, SPIRIT

1 is associated with consciousness, 5 is associated with Mercury, and 6 (1+5=6) is associated with Venus.

INNER CHILD SELF-PORTRAIT

This exercise requires major vulnerability. Create a portrait of the most wounded part of you. This can be in any artistic style you like, from drawing to collaging to something much more or less creative. Find a way to show your inner child and their needs, their feelings, the parts that feel the least acceptable to you. Illustrate them with compassion. Show their tenderness with the loving eyes of the one they need. When you look deeply at yourself through this lens of loving acceptance, what can you find? To aid you in your quest for radical self-compassion, we recommend doing a quiet meditation, listening to soothing sounds, and allowing space for your feelings, whatever they are. Allow this process to take the time it needs. Allow yourself to give yourself whatever you need here.

THE TOWER

When constructs we've built have served their purpose and become outdated, the Tower represents the need for immediate disassembly. Whether it's shifting relationships, spiritual paths, or careers, or major financial and lifestyle decisions, *change* is the name of the game. Many fear the Tower but the best we can do is to allow chaos and make room for change. Don't dig your heels in! There's no need to resist and no need to fear; you'll make it through this. The Tower is in the middle of the hero's journey! You're just about to get to the good part, but only if you allow everything to fall apart first. Trust yourself and the universe.

REVERSED: You're resisting a massive, integral change and it's causing chaos to reign in many aspects of your life. Remember, tender soul, that to resist change is to resist growth. It's painful to try to hold everything up when it wants to come tumbling down. Allow the breakdown so you can rebuild for the better.

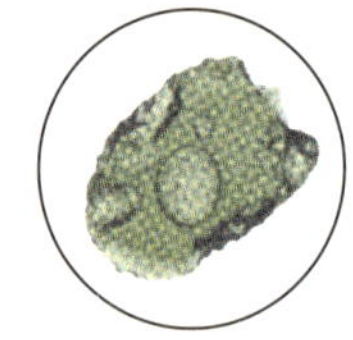

GEM

Moldavite

TRANSFORMATION, TRANSCENDENCE, CHAOS

This gem will help obliterate obstacles and create intense change.

SONG

"The Call"

REGINA SPEKTOR

SCENT

DUST AND ASHES

NUMEROLOGY

16

SELF-REFLECTION, STILLNESS, FOCUS

When broken down, 1 + 6 = 7, and 16 reminds us to pay attention to the divine nature in all things, even chaos.

HOW WE BLOOM

One of the most maligned cards in the deck, the Tower represents our old structures falling away as we ascend to new heights. Note the blooming of flowers representing fire in this card. While change may be intimidating, it often brings with it blessings we'd never otherwise know. Below, write down some hard-earned lessons that challenged you but were integral in the unfolding of your life. Embrace gratitude for your enduring spirit.

THE STAR

Even on the darkest of nights, there is a shimmer of light in the sky. Much like the ever-changing cycles of light and darkness in your life, the stars remain steady and glimmering. They are not always easy to see or feel, but within them there is hope and peace to be found.

Pause and look beyond whatever is clouding your connection to your higher self. Now is the time to connect with your inner voice, the calming heavenly space where clarity abounds. There is no need for action: Now is a time for revelry in hope and wonder, a peace found in unknowing, in just being. Rest under the light of the stars.

REVERSED: You may be finding yourself calling out to the universe, "What now? Where do I go from here?" What feels stale at this moment may feel like a punishment. But trust that this period is simply clarifying that pursuit of new purpose is necessary. Seek new inspiration, something you've never considered before.

GEM

Celestite

SUPERNATURAL GUIDANCE, INSIGHT, MEDITATION

Place this gem wherever you meditate, pray, and daydream to gain the clarity to seek.

SONG

"Visions"

JOSÉ GONZÁLEZ

SCENT

SLICK VINYL BOOTS AND SUN-WARMED DESERT ROCKS

NUMEROLOGY

17

HARMONY AND CELESTIAL INSPIRATION

As 1+7=8, the Star—like Strength—symbolizes balance.

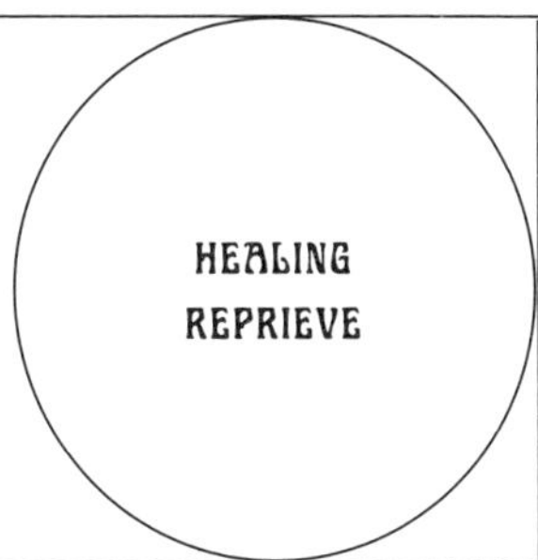

When we're feeling stuck, it can be hard to know what to do and where to go. The Star reminds us that sometimes, the best remedy is simply to rest. This activity's goal is to help you identify the blockages in your path as you recuperate and heal so that the next step you take is sure to be the right one.

NAME THE LIMITING BELIEFS THAT YOU CURRENTLY FEEL ARE HOLDING YOU BACK FROM TRULY REVELING IN YOUR AUTHENTIC SELF:

NOW LIST FIVE ACTIVITIES THAT FEEL LIKE REST FOR YOUR BODY, MIND, AND HEART:

1.
2.
3.
4.
5.

THIS WEEK, SEEK TO DO AT LEAST ONE OF THE ACTIVITIES ABOVE. THEN, JOURNAL ABOUT THE BENEFITS YOU GAIN FROM RESTING.

THE MOON

Things are not always as they seem. Be soft now. The Moon speaks to that which is both perpetually itself and constantly shifting. Are you looking at things as they are, or are you looking through rose-colored glasses? Are you projecting what you fear onto the situation at hand? Beware of your desire to paint the picture before you, and, instead, witness what might be presenting itself.

Remember, the Moon is all about reflection and inner wisdom, so seek truth. When in doubt, ask someone who can reflect the truth back to you, no matter how charged it may be. Approach inquiries with compassion—tenderness is a virtue. But so is the ability to be completely honest with yourself.

REVERSED: You are seeing things for what they are. Clear eyes, full heart! You know yourself and your intuition well now. You already know the answer. Don't doubt yourself.

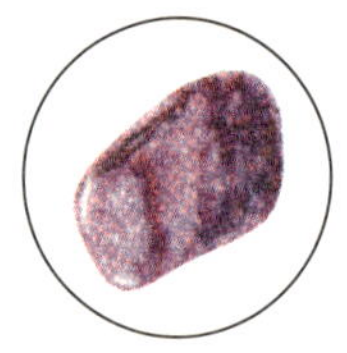

GEM

Sugilite

POSITIVITY, RELIEF, PEACE

Toe the line of reality and imagination with intention. Release all resistance.

SONG

"Moon Tattoo"

SOFI TUKKER

SCENT

COLD WATERFALLS ON MOSSY ROCKS

NUMEROLOGY

18

WISDOM, COMPLETION, CYCLES

As 1 + 8 = 9, this numerology also emphasizes the magic of development, hard work, and balance.

MOON WATER

Think of this as your own personal brand of holy water, the water you bless your most treasured items and yourself with when you want to feel supercharged with the mystique and magic of the moon.

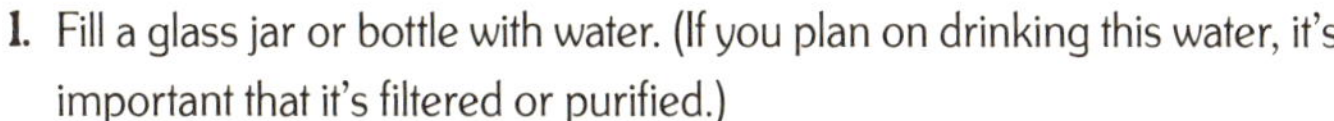

1. Fill a glass jar or bottle with water. (If you plan on drinking this water, it's important that it's filtered or purified.)
2. Leave it under the light of the moon to supercharge it with the mystical and positive energy of the moon. Consult the current stage of the moon cycle to see what energies are afoot.
3. If you do not plan to drink this water, add one or a few of your favorite crystals to the jar to boost the energy of whatever your crystals hold.
4. Bring the jar in before the sun rises and keep it wherever you most often sit in moments of meditation.
5. Use it in rituals and routines in your daily practice, adding a little to a bath during an evening of rest, cleansing your crystals when your energy feels lackluster and dull, or keeping it next to your bed to enhance your dreams.

A QUICK GUIDE:
A new moon (when it's totally dark and you can't see it) is associated with new beginnings, release, and attainment. A full moon is associated with high-powered celebration, healing, and manifestation. Generally, the two weeks following each of these two phases will include energies related to the ones listed here.

THE SUN

Wholeness, attainment, and success are shining upon you. You might be seeing the truth of a situation in which you'd previously been in the dark. What does everything look like when it's bathed in light? You could be getting what you want. Make sure you're not just looking at the bright side of things. The sun holds the contradiction of gentle, life-giving warmth and the violence of a raging ball of fire.

Consider your own opposing forces that some may not understand, but which you know to be strengths. Don't forget that life would cease if the burning, explosive sun were to disappear. Keep fueling your inner fire.

REVERSED: Your ability to see the good things in life is being blocked by clouds and fog. Consider shifting your perspective. Your gaze may be so focused upon the horizon that you are not taking in the beauty that already surrounds you.

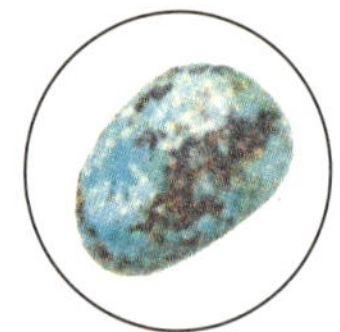

GEM

Turquoise
MOTIVATION, LUCK, VITALITY

Turquoise promotes energy and supports productivity. It also protects against outside influences and strengthens friendships.

SONG

"Here Comes the Sun"
THE BEATLES

SCENT

DAISIES ON A SUNNY WINDOWSILL

NUMEROLOGY

19
CYCLES, LIFE ON EARTH

The Sun can be related to both ten (1+9=10) and one (1+0=1). One can signify the first steps on a path, and 10 can be viewed as the completion of a cycle.

CONNECT WITH THE SUN

For the next ten days, write down a few notes about each day. You might choose to record your health, emotions, relationships, or any other standout pieces of your life. At the end of this ten-day period, notice what patterns have emerged. What cycles do you go through in just a week and a half? How does this relate to the Sun as an archetype? Record your findings below.

JUDGMENT

Do you feel a stirring in your soul? Judgment tells you that your inner world has grown or is about to. Brace for a thrilling spiritual adventure full of twists and turns—this will require a level head if you don't want to get dizzy. Consider this reassurance that you're on the right path. If, however, this card is surrounded by more fraught cards (indicating that you aren't seeing things clearly or perhaps that you're burdened with shame, doubt, or misperception), you may be missing some important lessons. Something within is longing to awaken.

REVERSED: How are you looking at your circumstance and how might you shift your perception? What changes can be made? Something about how you evaluate your life has gotten you off-track and you can't see the path to a fulfilling life from this standpoint. This is a great time to get outside advice.

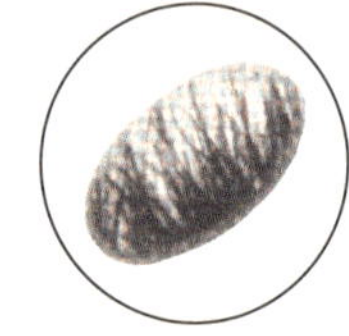

GEM

Tourmalinated quartz
SHIELDING, BALANCING, TRANSMUTATION

The positives and negatives are vital when considering resolution. Look at both sides of every story.

SONG

"Power On"
JAMES BLAKE

SCENT

LEMONS AND VINEGAR

NUMEROLOGY

20
DUALITY, BONDS, CONTRAST

Look to the Empress and Justice's numerology to gain insight about interpreting this card's amplified power.

IMAGINATIVE LISTENING

Locate an object you feel spiritually connected to. This could be a crystal, your tarot deck, a religious icon, or anything that stirs a feeling of connection to the universe or whatever you consider divine. Examine this object and notice the tiny details. How does it feel against your fingertips? What does it smell like? What's the best way to describe its coloring, its weight, the way it looks in the light?

After you've fully witnessed this object, close your eyes and imagine it coming to life. Breathe deeply.

Ask your object for wisdom. If nothing comes up, ask it questions. *What do I need to know about my life right now? In the face of adversity, what should I do? When I'm stuck on my path, how do I move forward?* What does your object have to say?

THE WORLD

We find ourselves in the liminal place that is the end of the beginning and the beginning of the end. As the Fool, we've completed our journey. Lessons have been learned. Hardship has presented itself and we've persevered. The edge of one universe is a portal into the next. Feel pride in all the work you've done and humbly take a step through to become the Fool once again—only this time, seasoned with all you've just learned. You're ready. You're deserving. You are radiantly, magically human.

REVERSED: Don't hold back just because the unknown is intimidating. Your new motto? "Be scared, do it anyway!" You may find that holding on to pleasant feelings is a lot more comfortable than embracing an uncertain future, but it's not going to serve you in the long run. Allow cycles to end. Allow cycles to begin. The universe will continue moving, whether you release your anxiety about it all or not. The old Zen proverb says it best: Let go or be dragged.

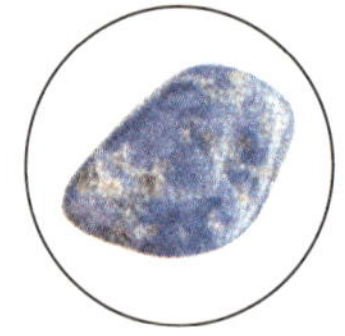

GEM

Sodalite

INTELLECTUALISM, COMPLETION, TRUST

Enhance trust in oneself with this gem that stimulates rational thought, intuition, and effective communication.

SONG

"Fade Into You"

MAZZY STAR

SCENT

POLISHED WOOD FLOORS AND A NEW SUITCASE

NUMEROLOGY

21

ALIGNMENT, BELONGING, COMMUNITY

Lucky and extremely favorable, this number embodies curiosity, exuberance, and achievement.

YOUR WORLD

The world is the combination of every piece of your life and lessons learned. If you are the world, what makes up your card? Put your name, photo, or self-portrait in the center of the circle below, then add all the pieces of your world around that circle. People, experiences, songs—anything goes. This is *your* world card. What does it look like?

The

Minor Arcana

INTRODUCTION TO THE MINORS

The Minor Arcana represents the stuff of everyday life. This is not to say these fifty-six cards are at all banal; they are more immediate, temporary, and perhaps simpler in essence (but what in life ever feels simple?).

This section of the tarot speaks to the cycles of everyday life: money, home, family, love, work, ideas, creativity . . . the things that make our lives uniquely ours. While the Major cards deal with big themes of existence, the Minors are all about the human experience on the terrestrial level. They help us keep things in perspective; while the most painful moments of our lives may be temporary—and the cards remind us that it is all just part of the cycle—so too are the highest of highs. Life is not about feeling good all the time. Life is about being. The Minors ask us to be present with whatever is in the here and now because each moment is inherently divine, once in a lifetime.

Consider the Minor Arcana a series of snapshots from the road trip of life. Seek the connections between these cards and yourself. Notice the memories they stir up and remember to stay present. Everything is temporary.

Wands

ELEMENTAL CONNECTION: Fire
EMBODIMENT: Inner Energy and Life Source

Blazing brightly, the Wands illuminate the driving forces of our lives—passion, creativity, inspiration, and the root of our energy. Fire signs Aries, Leo, and Sagittarius might feel a warmth toward these cards. When viewed as staffs or weapons, the Wands can be considered unfavorable, but as beauty is in the eye of the beholder, so too are the branches depicted in the suit of Wands. Are they wands—tools of creation and manifestation? Or staffs—means of warding off enemies or even beating down the competition? Look through the flames and into the coals that warm the hearth of our existence to see that one cannot exist without the other.

CONCEPTS TO EXPLORE WITH THE SUIT OF WANDS:

- ○ *Igniting our inner fire*
- ○ *Flashes of inspiration*
- ○ *Energetic spiritual connections*
- ○ *Curiosity about the unnamable and intangible*

CONNECT WITH WANDS: *Visualize a fire in your belly and take a deep, slow breath in through your nose. Imagine your breath stoking that inner fire, fanning its flames so that it grows brighter and hotter. Breathe with just as much intention as you exhale through the mouth and repeat. This exercise promotes oxygen flow in the body and reduces stress while also tapping into the energy of the Wands!*

LIST YOUR CREATIVITY

Think about how each card has many different interpretations behind it. We see three different tools depicted in the Three of Wands, for example. These are tools that can be used to create (building furniture or a home) or destroy (disassembling a child's crib once they outgrow it, or even as a crude means of breaking a window). Creativity is not just about art; it's in our ability to change the world around us. Find creative interpretations of each card's image and list your observations below.

ACE: ______

TWO: ______

THREE: ______

FOUR: ______

FIVE: ______

SIX: ______

SEVEN: ______

EIGHT: ______

NINE: ______

TEN: ______

APPRENTICE: ______

CHAMPION: ______

ORACLE: ______

ELDER: ______

TAKE IT FURTHER

Consider a particularly intense experience in your personal life. Something that was so substantial that there's no escaping its power. Perhaps it's a beautiful memory or experience such as giving birth to a child or winning an award for your life's work. Or, you might think back to something terrible, such as a heartbreak. Try to see the positives *and* negatives of your experience. When we use a balanced lens, we may better appreciate each part of our story and integrate these memories fully.

ACE OF WANDS

You are made of pure, divine energy. Everything you do is sacred. A wand is a lightning bolt crackling with energy. The ace represents becoming. Manifestation. Creation. The Ace of Wands is a declaration that everything is ritual, everything is holy, every little thing you do is magic.

Ask yourself: *What energy is calling me to action right now?* Connect with your inner fire by taking action in the physical realm. The wisdom held within will be revealed.

REVERSED: Are you doubting yourself or feeling a bit of impostor syndrome? Perhaps something is blocking your creative potential . . . and that block may be coming from inside. Pull a clarifying card to identify what else is going on or what will help you overcome this blockage. Trust your intrinsic value, you are worthy.

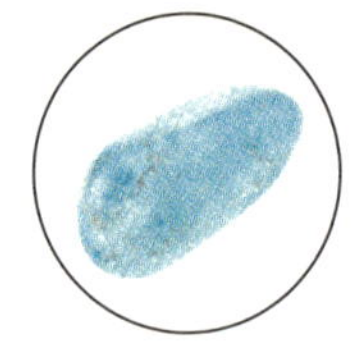

GEM

Aquamarine
INITIATION, TEMPERANCE, HOPE

SONG

"Wide Open Spaces"
SOCCER MOMMY

SCENT

A FIELD OF GRAINS AND DRIED GRASSES

Write down your most common creative block (e.g., self-doubt, ADHD, lack of resources, etc.) and consider what tools might help you move through the stagnancy. Brainstorm ideas and create pathways through inaction to use when you don't feel the energy flowing.

CREATIVE BLOCK BUSTERS

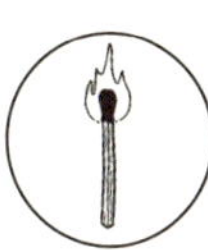

TWO OF WANDS

GEM

Zebra jasper
ENERGY, BIG PLANS, SOOTHING FEARS

SONG

"Head Underwater"
JENNY LEWIS

SCENT

A SWIMMING POOL

There are major choices to be made. Perhaps the hardest part is knowing that any outcome has negatives *and* positives. So how do you make a decision? Being present with yourself can clarify the situation at hand, so consider what you might need to regulate your body, mind, emotions, or any conflicting states of being. How does your body feel when you think about the options you're faced with? What does your intuition tell you? Consult a friend if you need outside advice; just make sure to ask someone who knows how to tell the truth and not just what you might want to hear.

REVERSED: Have you been avoiding a substantial decision? Whatever avoidance is plaguing you, this is your nudge to stop waiting around and just make a move. You already know the pros and cons. Don't waste any more time in avoidance. The time for action is now.

COMBINE ENERGY FOR CLARITY

Hold a ritual fire with a trusted friend. It could be in person, making a (safe) bonfire, or over a video call using candles in your respective spaces. Light the fire with the intention to provide light to cast out the shadows of doubt and illuminate the path ahead. Speak your fears and hesitations aloud. Offer them to the fire and watch them burn away. Close the ritual by thanking the fire and your friend for supporting your well-being.

THREE OF WANDS

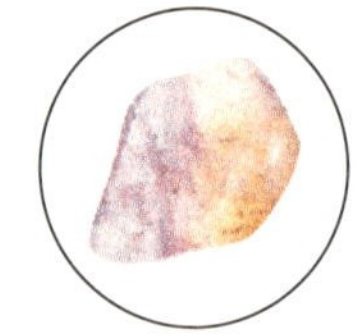

GEM

Ametrine
SELF-CONFIDENCE, MENTAL STABILITY, TENSION RELIEF

SONG

"The Bug Collector"
HALEY HEYNDERICKX

SCENT

ARNICA, CAMPHOR, AND PEPPERMINT OILS

All the efforts you've put into positive creative and career endeavors are paying off—finally! You are rooted in a place of safety and your mind is clear. Now is a great time to prepare for the future, to look ahead knowing that some challenges can be prepared for with foresight, especially since you are currently in a steady space. And remember, you are not on the journey alone. Your path ahead is meant to be in communion with others, separate but forging on beside one another.

REVERSED: Just because you have invested a lot in opportunities, relationships, or plans that aren't panning out, doesn't mean you have wasted your time. Consider how these moments add value to your understanding of yourself.

GATHER YOUR WANDS

Wands can be seen as tools of our trades. Identify three ways you create, then select three objects to serve as your "wands." A writer might choose their favorite pen, a painter might choose a brush, and a chef might choose a wooden spoon. Don't sell yourself short, either: We are *all* creative in many ways in our day-to-day lives.

Display these objects in special places or create a piece of art featuring their likenesses.

FOUR OF WANDS

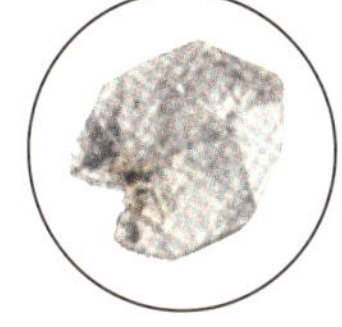

GEM

Herkimer diamond
ATTUNEMENT, HOLINESS, GUIDANCE

SONG

"Thank You"
DIDO

SCENT

FRESH-SQUEEZED ORANGE JUICE

You've worked so hard to get here, and finally you've triumphed over something major. It's time to celebrate! Appreciate the labor it took to get you to this finish line. Give yourself and all those involved some thanks. Make the time and space to revel in feelings of joy, safety, and love! Cozy up with your favorite people and toast each other. You've earned it!

REVERSED: Any upset or roadblock happening right now may feel like a challenge, but it's merely a small detour on your journey. Take the difficulty of this moment and consider it proof of devotion as you keep your eyes on the road ahead. Don't lose sight of what you're after—just get to it.

MINDFUL CONSUMPTION

As you sit down to a meal today, consider the many hands and resources it took for this food to arrive at your table. Imagine each person who touched your produce, grains, herbs, all of it—from the farmer who planted the seed to the grocery store clerk who stocked the shelves and the hands that created the meal before you. Send a mental note of gratitude to each of these people and consider how you might be able to meet the world with deep gratitude today.

FIVE OF WANDS

The Five of Wands calls us to respond to things that confuse or irritate us with curiosity. Just because something is different, it does not mean it is bad. Instead of immediately reacting negatively to something that challenges your current understanding of the world, approach this newness with curiosity. Personal growth is an asset. Whatever feels like an affront to the person you are and how you live your life, think of it as a teacher instead.

REVERSED: You're avoiding something, aren't you? If you face it, you're guaranteed a solution. Of course, with any sort of conflict, there is the chance that you won't get your way, but more often than not, when you show up willing to engage, to stay in conflict until it transforms to resolution, you will find yourself empowered with new information. Save it for later use.

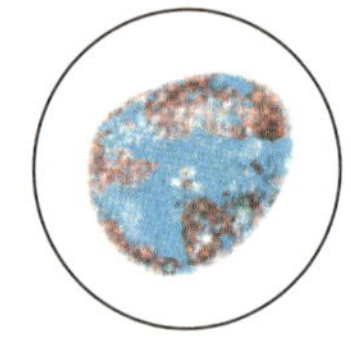

GEM

Chrysocolla
COMMUNICATION, REWIRING PATHWAYS, COURAGE

SONG

"The Hardest Button to Button"
THE WHITE STRIPES

SCENT

RUBBER BANDS AND A FRESH PAIR OF SCISSORS

BRAINSPOTTING

Brainspotting is a simple somatic practice that uses eye movement to locate and lessen stress, sadness, or worry in your brain. It helps to shake off negative experiences that linger in your body when you think of them.

In 2013, the psychotherapist David Grand discovered that "where you look affects how you feel. Brainspotting locates points in the client's visual field that help to access unprocessed trauma in the subcortical brain." Visit brainspotting.com to learn more.

SIX OF WANDS

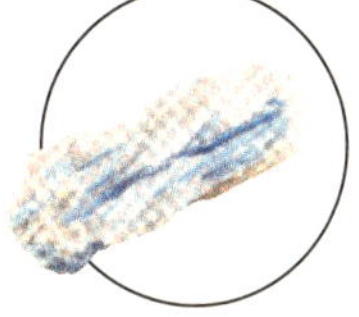

GEM

Kyanite
POSITIVITY, HARMONY, EMERGENCE

SONG

"Lucky Sometimes"
POKEY LAFARGE

SCENT

CARAMEL AND HONEY

You've got quite a good reason to be proud! And if success hasn't shown up yet, it's just around the corner. You've toiled to coordinate your strengths and talents and your efforts have paid off. This card gives you permission to shout your success from the rooftops! Be assertive, tell the people you love that you want to celebrate how far you've come and how hard you've worked to get here. Keep in mind, you're not at the finish line yet, but right now you deserve to party!

REVERSED: You've gained some success, but you'd prefer to keep it quiet for now. This moment isn't about glory, but redefining what success means to you. Society's standard for success isn't the same as your own, and that's okay. Once you've crafted your own definition, you're destined to thrive. Remember, what society views as "failure" or a "fall from grace" may be a blessing to you.

REDEFINING SUCCESS

When it comes to work and career, it can be challenging to create our own definition of success. When we craft our own concept of what "achievement" looks like, it becomes easier to embrace our own accomplishments.

Use a journal or separate sheet of paper to write down three things you value above your career, three lesser-acknowledged things you view as a success, and three ways you can celebrate these accomplishments.

SEVEN OF WANDS

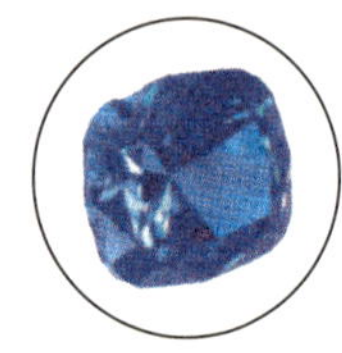

GEM

Sapphire
PROTECTION, CONFIDENCE, ANCIENT WISDOM

SONG

"Under the Table"
FIONA APPLE

SCENT

CINNAMON, CLOVES, AND GINGER

Right when you feel like you're at the top of your game, someone else has to spoil it with their insecurities, projections, and false assumptions. When you stand out in a crowd, others will inevitably be drawn to you, for better or for worse. You may hold an opinion that others call counterculture or controversial. But if you believe in it, stick to it. Hold strong in your opinions even when others disagree. Your opinion is valid, too. Trust the wisdom of experience to push forward.

REVERSED: You have grown up in a community with a lot of critical voices. You are used to having to fight for your opinion to be heard and you're exhausted. Stop wasting your energy convincing others of something they are not willing to accept and instead, hold your power by accepting yourself as you are.

Studies show that if there has been *one* person in your life who has advocated for you and your dreams, you have a far higher chance of being a capable, resilient, and successful person than those without support. As an adult, you have the capacity to keep building your support team. List out the people you can trust to hype you up and support you in all endeavors.

YOUR HYPE CREW

EIGHT OF WANDS

GEM

Lemurian quartz
AWAKENING, CHANGE, SUDDEN MOVEMENT

SONG

"Dancing in the Dark"
LUCY DACUS

SCENT

A STRUCK MATCH

Change is in the air and the feeling of forward momentum is palpable. The path ahead is illuminated and you're ready for some serious change. Whether it's achieving goals, pursuing new ideas, or traveling somewhere you've never been, there's a burst of energy begging to let loose—so let it. If you find yourself feeling intimidated by the changes you face, remember that change is not always difficult, and even if it is, difficulty isn't inherently a bad thing. Don't let nerves tempt you to tamp down your enthusiasm. You have every reason to believe you will succeed.

REVERSED: You may be forging ahead when what you need is to simmer for a moment. Take a breath and do some grounding exercises so you can move forward strategically instead of trying to get things done too quickly. See if you can gain fresh perspective to take with you on the coming adventure.

PACKING LIST

Moving forward in your life, what do you want to bring along, and what should stay in the past? Make two columns. In one, list what you're keeping and in the other, list all the things you are leaving behind.

Ritualize it! Now that you have your lists of what is coming along and going away, create a piece of art from this information in any way you see fit.

NINE OF WANDS

You've been fighting so hard and you are *tired.* Recognize your weariness while acknowledging that the battle is not finished. Traditionally, this card shows a wounded soldier leaning on their weapon, standing alone among a group of other fighting tools. But it's important we note that the weapons here are the Wands. What inner fire can you conjure to finish this fight? It's time to dig deep and bolster yourself for the final blows—you've got this. Remember that when fighting for yourself, it's about staying one step ahead. When fighting on behalf of a relationship or team, it isn't about winning—it's about understanding. Use your wands well!

REVERSED: Stubbornness is keeping you from ending this fight. Are you stuck in righteousness? Are you afraid to act because it may lead to heartache, loss, or instability? Taking the first step is the only way forward. It's time.

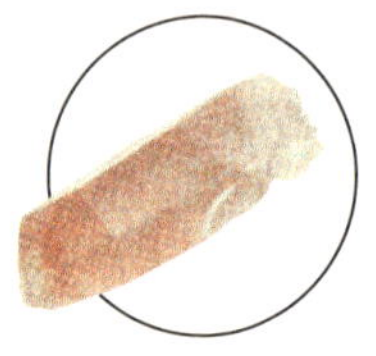

GEM

Lithium quartz
HOLISTIC SUPPORT, EASE, NURTURING

SONG

"SUPERBLOOM"
MISTERWIVES

SCENT

AMBER

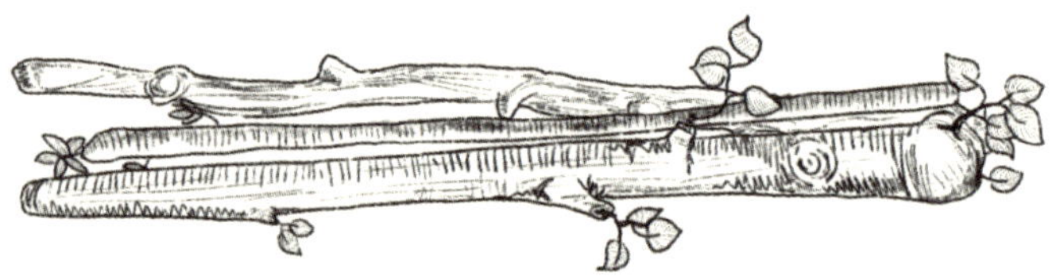

THE BATTLE WORTH FIGHTING

Journal about the battles you've been fighting in your life and the lessons you've learned along the way. When you think about where things started and who you were then versus where it all stands now, both within and outside of yourself, how have you grown? Reflect on the path and see what new information you find.

TEN OF WANDS

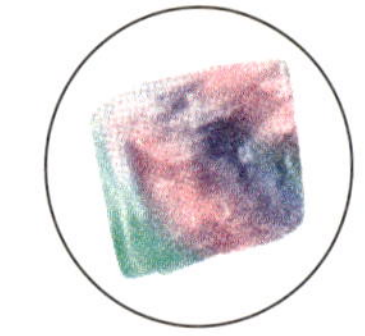

GEM

Fluorite
FOCUS, CLEAR VISION, AWARENESS

SONG

"Lost Track"
HAIM

SCENT

GRAPEFRUIT SELTZER

Tens tend to represent the completion of a suit, and now you, the querent, are standing at the threshold, holding the weight of the lessons you've learned along the way. This card comes up in times of intense grief and in times of relief. Perhaps you are living with the impact of a wise, ultimately positive decision that has also come with great pain. Paradoxically, gratitude and grief can happen at the same time. It makes sense to feel disoriented. Wisdom can come with a cost, but that does not make it any less valuable.

REVERSED: Are you stuck in a cycle of pain? You may be shifting the blame from yourself to others, not taking enough of the burden and responsibility on yourself. This is a reckoning to get honest with yourself and own your part of the story. That is the only way to move forward.

GRATITUDE FOR THE GRIND

It might be tempting to focus on the burdens this card represents in your life. Regardless of your current situation, mindfulness can help foster gratitude and prevent a future resentment.

Identify the biggest struggle or challenge you're currently facing and journal about it. Ask yourself: *Why am I performing this duty? What gifts does this "burden" bring to my life and how am I growing from it? Is this something I truly must take on, and if so, why is it beneficial to my life? What can I learn from this?*

Rather than trying to force gratitude, choose curiosity instead. Explore the topic, your feelings, and what can be gained from the part you're currently playing.

APPRENTICE OF WANDS

All signs are pointing to *hell yes*. This card represents the student of passion itself and an openness to learning, jumping in, and showing vigor in whatever is to come. There is a great enthusiasm for the sensual, sexual, and creative aspects of the fiery Wands. Enthusiasm is not to be contained! Either your energies are initiating a mastery of sorts, or there is good news on the way.

REVERSED: Something is getting in the way of your self-expression. If you sense someone in your life may be withholding or deceitful, this reversal asks you to trust your instinct. To doubt your intuitive power is to bottle your entire self. Trust your inner knowledge.

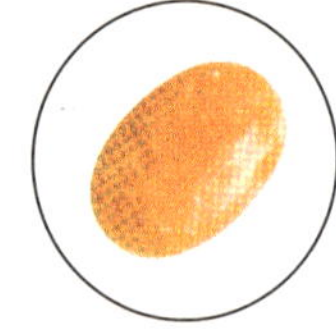

GEM

Orange calcite
PASSION, VISIONS, PHYSICAL AND EMOTIONAL ALIGNMENT

SONG

"This Is Your Life"
HANNAH COHEN

SCENT

PASSIONFRUIT, GUAVA, AND MANGO

SNAPSHOT OF POWER

In this moment when you are fully feeling the heights (or depths) of your power, take note. What do you notice about your world currently? Create a "snapshot" of what has helped you get to this point by journaling the factors that have affected your self-expression and experience right now. Reflecting on these things can help us decide how we want to move forward, whether by creating rituals and habits out of our behaviors or by changing something that isn't working.

CHAMPION OF WANDS

The Champion of Wands is here to turn the Apprentice's inspiration into reality! Gallop full-force toward your dreams with your passion, energy, and practical skills. Taking calculated risks will catapult you into a new realm of learning. Do you want to follow this path alone or bring others along? Stay mindful of your impulses and be aware of your own hunger to jump ahead. Make sure to bolster your joyful energy with practicality.

REVERSED: You're bursting with energy. You may be excited to channel it into a personal project or you might feel a little directionless. Either way, your energy is meant to fulfill *you*. Decide how to utilize all that's bubbling up to invigorate your inner world and personal development. Just avoid short-term impulses. This energy is meant to be sustained.

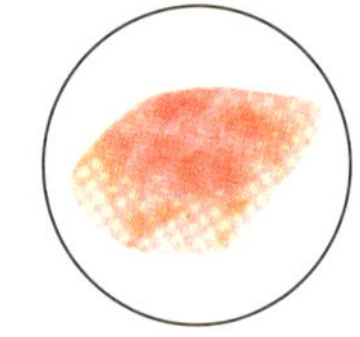

GEM

Sunstone
STAMINA, VITALITY, ADVENTUROUSNESS

SONG

"Wow"
BECK

SCENT

GREEN TEA

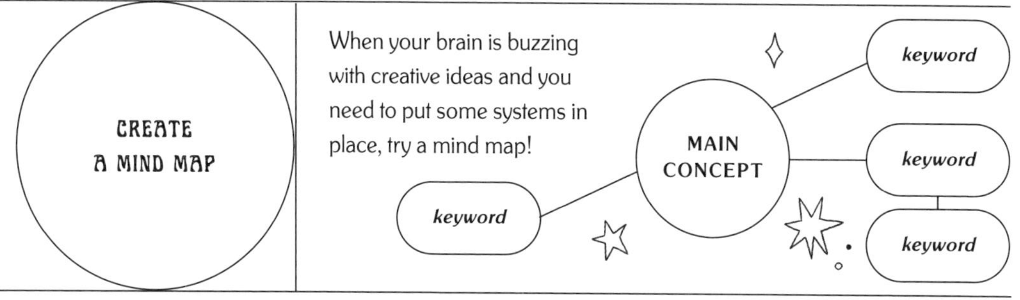

1. Write your main concept in the center of a page. If you'd like, you can draw a bubble around this to keep it neat.
2. Add keywords around your central idea (drawing bubbles around them if you'd like), connecting them back to your main concept with lines. Keep these keywords brief.
3. Color-code each line, or branch, according to theme, emotion, etc. so you can easily see how the paths connect and support your big idea.
4. Add images around your branches. Your brain will be more likely to ping with activity with the inclusion of inspiring visuals!

ORACLE OF WANDS

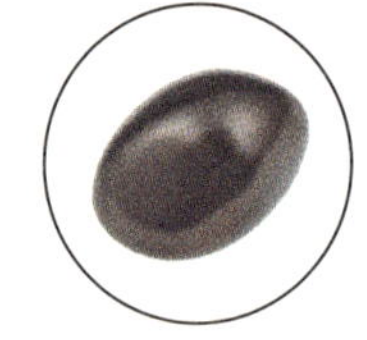

GEM

Jet
EMPATHY, FORCEFULNESS, DOMINANCE

SONG

"The Mother"
BRANDI CARLILE

SCENT

VETIVER AND AN OLD PATCHWORK QUILT

You are a divine instrument, a social butterfly so skilled in making connections and putting yourself out there, it's remarkable. You've taken the hardships of your life and used them to become one powerful being. You like being the center of attention, and with all that you've overcome, you deserve it! People are drawn to your zest for life and the dark humor that helps others see the depth behind your shine. Keep loving every aspect of you, from the shiny exterior to the shadow self that holds so much insight into who you are.

REVERSED: You're feeling more introverted than usual, but it's just what you need as you start to see your own self-worth. You've lacked confidence in the recent past, but this time alone has you connecting more deeply with yourself than ever before. It seems you've found your inner fire and fuel.

HONEY JAR

Write your name on a slip of paper and gather small tokens that represent everything that makes you special. Try rose quartz for the abundant love you have within, and cinnamon sticks for your spicy energy. Place everything in a jar and cover with honey or something equally sweet. Place this jar under your bed with the intention of infusing every night's sleep with radiant love for yourself and others.

ELDER OF WANDS

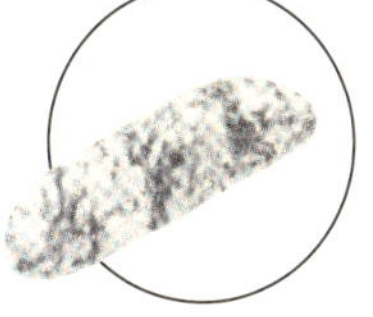

GEM

Magnesite
INTELLECT, MEDITATIVE POWER, RESPONSIBILITY

SONG

"Keep On Keeping On"
CURTIS MAYFIELD

SCENT

A GIANT, CRACKLING BONFIRE

This charismatic and magnetic Elder has learned to listen to every vibration of their surroundings and make plans accordingly. They enlist the help of others to implement their plans, and others are more than happy to help, as there's a collective belief in the Elder's visionary abilities. This card represents someone who is capable of maturely assessing a situation, delegating tasks, and leaving a legacy. It speaks to vitality, moral virtue, and knowing when to shed old skin and when to nest.

REVERSED: Insecurity has laid its beady little eyes on your situation. Whether it's you or someone else, there's a deep tension resulting in a sort of stalemate. This could be due to conflict avoidance or ego, and you must use the resources you have to pull the hidden shadows to the light. Address whatever is keeping you in this unsavory place.

ASSEMBLE YOUR COURT

One of the most enriching things we can do is express gratitude. It can strengthen our lives from the bottom up, especially when we share it.

Write a letter to each of the most influential, supportive, and loving people in your life thanking them for their presence. Give them this gift free of expectation for reciprocation.

Cups

ELEMENTAL CONNECTION: Water
EMBODIMENT: Our Emotions

CONNECT WITH CUPS:
Practice bilateral tapping to calm stormy waters of emotion. Lightly tap back and forth (with a finger or two) on the left part of your body and then the right, perhaps on either side of your head or both shoulders. Tap your feet back and forth, or look left and right. You can activate and integrate information from your brain's two hemispheres, creating a fluid and soothing sensation amid any emotional ups and downs.

In the suit of Cups, we see a reflection of our innermost feelings. Water signs Cancer, Scorpio, and Pisces may identify with themes of fluidity and the emotional depth in this suit. Traditionally, Cups are considered favorable, as they are so often associated with some of the juiciest parts of living. But of course, feeling anything can be just as much a difficulty as a joy—this is the suit of the heart, so it is also the suit of emotional anguish. No one suit is better than another and none is without its ups and downs. Like liquid, the Cups are slippery. Waves of emotion are a powerful thing to hold and embody. Flow with it all.

CONCEPTS TO EXPLORE WITH THE SUIT OF CUPS:

- ○ *Allowing emotions to flow through you*
- ○ *Observing waves of feeling and watching them pass by*
- ○ *Exploring your own fluidity*
- ○ *Quenching your emotional thirst*

LIST YOUR EMOTIONS

Take a look through the pages that follow, specifically at the Cups cards' artwork. From the open blossom of the Ace's flower to the magical deep-sea creatures of the Oracle and Elder, what feelings come up within when you examine these images? You might identify emotions like *sadness*, *joy*, or *warmth*, or physical feelings like *tingling*, *cold feet*, *racing heart*. In the blanks on this page, write out any emotions you feel when looking through the art. Refer back to this page as a key to understanding your personal insights into this suit.

ACE: ______

TWO: ______

THREE: ______

FOUR: ______

FIVE: ______

SIX: ______

SEVEN: ______

EIGHT: ______

NINE: ______

TEN: ______

APPRENTICE: ______

CHAMPION: ______

ORACLE: ______

ELDER: ______

TAKE IT FURTHER

Journal about how these emotions and sensations might manifest as actions. For example, *When I feel my feet getting cold, I know to light the fireplace*, or *When my heart skips a beat and I'm feeling emotionally tender, I can text my loved ones that I am thinking about them.* By pairing our emotions or a physical sensation with planned actions, we can combat negative impulsivity and reactivity by choosing mindfulness.

Ace of Cups

GEM

Rose quartz
UNCONDITIONAL LOVE, TENDERNESS, BEGINNINGS

SONG

"I Love Every Little Thing About You"
SYREETA

SCENT

VANILLA CANDLES AND CANDY HEARTS

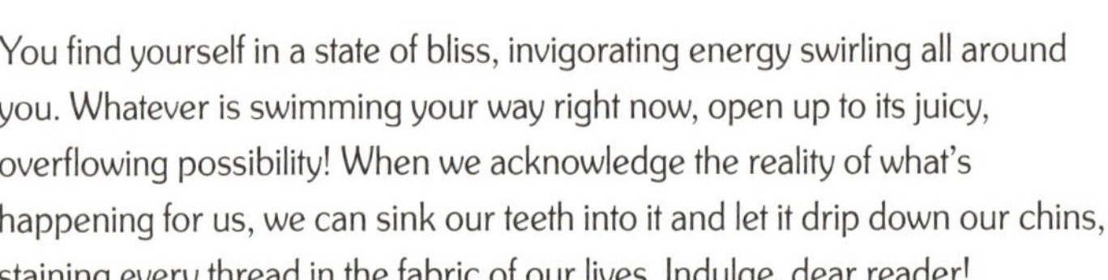

You find yourself in a state of bliss, invigorating energy swirling all around you. Whatever is swimming your way right now, open up to its juicy, overflowing possibility! When we acknowledge the reality of what's happening for us, we can sink our teeth into it and let it drip down our chins, staining every thread in the fabric of our lives. Indulge, dear reader!

REVERSED: Take this as a sign that you are in the right place emotionally. You may not be expressing it outwardly, but that's not necessary right now. This is the time to connect with your subconscious mind and trust your intuition. Your internal world is ripe and ready for you to bite into it however you please—don't hesitate to do this *your* way.

INVOKING LOVE

Our emotions are chemical. When we "feel" love, we're experiencing a flood of chemicals which, when paired with our concepts of relationships, create what we've all agreed to call "love." The chemicals involved are predominantly oxytocin and dopamine. While we often think of falling in love as requiring another person and a lot of luck, we can create the sensation of love (and, if we think of ourselves as our own best partner, love itself) by invoking the emotion ourselves.

Use a combination of the tasks below to tap into the spirit of love and this card. Drink up!

DOPAMINE	OXYTOCIN
The Reward Chemical	*The Love Hormone*
Completing a task	Playing with a pet, baby, or child
Eating food that feels good	Giving compliments
Sleeping	Eye contact
Writing gratitude lists	Skin-to-skin contact
Listening to music	Volunteering
Sensual pleasure	Sensual pleasure

Two of Cups

The Two of Cups speaks to a profound connection—one that is expansive, balanced, and rooted both spiritually and physically. The two forces in this image work in harmony toward common goals. Passion and compassion in equal measure. This card may be related to romance, but it can also indicate a beautiful friendship full of mutual understanding. This is a connection that can withstand anything and has the strength to go the distance.

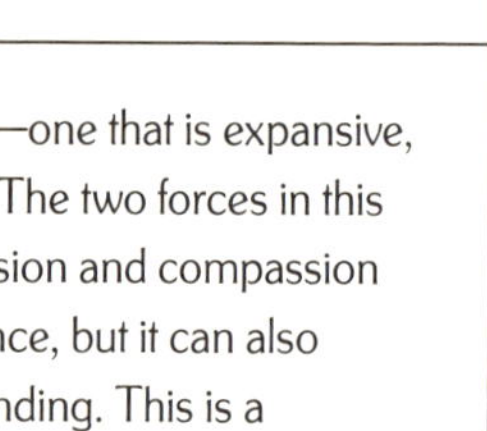

REVERSED: A miscommunication of sorts has occurred. It may be a misunderstanding of the investment of each party involved in a particular relationship, or perhaps it's a simple misinterpretation, a faulty assumption. Whatever's happening, there is a lack of balance.

GEM

Hiddenite
ROMANCE, PURE CONNECTION, GLOWING

SONG

"Right Down the Line"
LUCIUS

SCENT

A DUSTY VINTAGE LOVE LETTER

CHECKS AND BALANCES

Write an exhaustive list of all the responsibilities in your home and workspace. Then, identify who is responsible for each item.

Does the division of labor make sense? Is it fair, equitable, does it feel good? If rebalancing needs to happen, use this moment to start the conversations.

RESPONSIBILITY	PERSON RESPONSIBLE

THREE OF CUPS

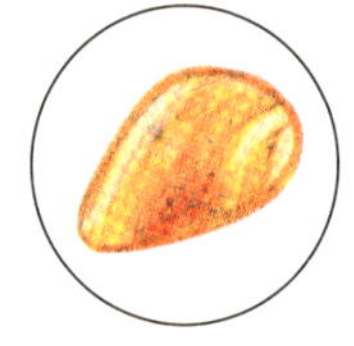

GEM

Amber
FRIENDSHIP, CUDDLES, SWEETNESS

SONG

"Best Friend"
SAWEETIE (FEATURING DOJA CAT)

SCENT

DEEP RED WINE

This is a moment of pure vibrancy. Friends, family, and lovers abound, and you feel unstoppable. You're inspired, fulfilled, and it's time to dance! Right now, your gratitude is bubbling over. Allow the fullness of this moment to take up every ounce of your attention; everything is temporary, so make sure to soak up as much of this beauty as possible. The Three of Cups is about celebrating every moment, big and small.

REVERSED: Are you so surrounded by beloveds that you aren't getting enough downtime? Have you been socializing or partying a little too hard? Take a moment to enjoy sweet solitude. Alternately, if you're struggling to feel fulfilled socially, consider the patterns you might put an end to. How might that feel?

THREE CUPS OF LOVE

Label three jars or envelopes: 1. COMMUNITY, 2. BELOVEDS, 3. SELF. In each, deposit scraps of paper with notes of gratitude about that particular relationship. Inside jokes, memories, quirks, whatever you love and appreciate.

Whenever you need a reminder of how full your cups are, pull a slip from each and feel into your network of support from the inside out.

FOUR OF CUPS

GEM

Topaz
FIRE, PASSION, LASER FOCUS

SONG

"(I Can't Get No) Satisfaction"
THE ROLLING STONES

SCENT

DIRTY SHEETS

The universe just keeps handing you more and more opportunities—and yet, something doesn't feel right. You're likely aware of your own good fortune, but there's a sense of hollowness that can't be filled. You want the *juice* of the human experience. It's time to recognize what isn't working so you can find what makes you feel most alive. Seek out the unfathomable. Open yourself to the mystery of life. In the words of Cheryl Strayed, "Put yourself in the way of beauty."

REVERSED: Stop hiding—you're ready to open up and be vulnerable again. Avoiding hardship also means avoiding the beautiful and spectacular experiences the world has to offer. Be scared and excited at once. Take a risk.

DO IT SCARED

The thing that often holds us back in life is a fear of the great what-if. What if it doesn't go well? What if it *does* go well?

The Four of Cups is an indicator that you know what to pursue . . . but the potential for what-ifs might feel enormous. Consider what would truly make you feel alive. Then, shove the what-ifs out the window and do it. Book the plane ticket. Find a new job. Apply for that grant. Whatever it is, do the damn thing, and do it scared if you have to.

FIVE OF CUPS

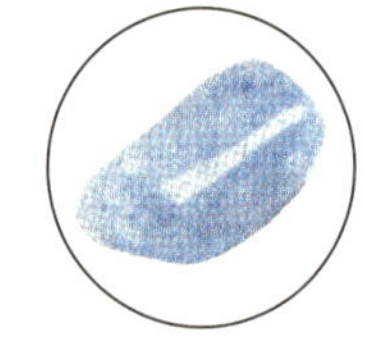

You are in your feels. And look, it's valid: Your pain is real. But this card is asking you to put a timer on your wallowing, because you're starting to get stuck in the stormy sea of the past. Pull that heavy anchor up from the depths so you can sail forward and realize your fullest potential. New possibilities are on the horizon. Once that little crack of light from the future shines on your face, you'll look back at this moment and think, *Why did I waste all that time wallowing when I had this present to look forward to?* Check that timer, let it ding, and step into a better state of being.

REVERSED: You're blaming yourself for something that didn't turn out well. Call on a friend for their honest perspective. Staying alone with these thoughts will only cause a self-shaming spiral. You're on the path to discovering how to open your heart and take risks again, so trust that this setback is simply data necessary to make different decisions in the future.

GEM

Blue quartz
PERSPECTIVE, COMMUNICATION, RELEASE

SONG

"The Wind"
CAT STEVENS

SCENT

GRAVEYARD DIRT

MAKE INVISIBLE INK

Write out the pains you feel are holding you back in invisible ink. Mix two tablespoons of water with two tablespoons of baking soda, dip a cotton swab or toothpick into the mixture, and write out your big feels on a piece of paper. As it dries, think of your pain leaving your body and dissolving with this soda-and-water mixture. Dip a sponge or new cotton swab in grape juice and "paint" over the secret message to reveal it. Shed the hidden words where you plan to never return. Release it to move forward.

SIX OF CUPS

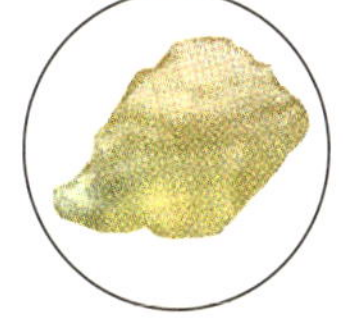

GEM

Libyan gold tektite
ENTHUSIASM, DESIRE, PLAY

SONG

"This Is a Photograph"
KEVIN MORBY

SCENT

STICKY, SUN-BAKED LEMONADE

Sweet childhood memories are streaming back as you enter a time of contemplation. Your mind is alive with the joys of simplicity, the pleasure found in newness and curiosity. People from the past may be reentering your life, triggering fond daydreams about what once was. Use this time to pursue refreshing new experiences that echo tender moments from the past. Build present purpose within nostalgia and allow it to fuel new creative expression and curiosity for the present.

REVERSED: There's an unmet need to live in the present, and this card is asking you to stop trying to fix the past. You might be stuck on a certain memory or heartache and it's time to figure out how to let go. Hype yourself up to face it and trust you will move on.

THE PAST IS SMOKE

This is a good moment to sit still and journal. Consider what pieces of your past warm you with nostalgia and what might be distracting you from the present. Write three full pages about what's been on your mind. Decide what's working and what isn't and make a plan to release what no longer serves you. Rewrite what you want to let go of and burn that piece of paper (safely!). Say "bye-bye" to what you no longer need and watch the smoke blow away.

SEVEN OF CUPS

GEM

Barite
DISCERNMENT, AWARENESS, DIVINE WILL

SONG

"Maps"
YEAH YEAH YEAHS

SCENT

A BUFFET PILED HIGH WITH YOUR FAVORITE FOODS

Temptation might be hiding around the corner as you navigate your chosen path. Distractions draw your attention away from your heart-centered work. In this moment, it's easy to find yourself torn between authenticity and self-sabotage. Remove yourself from the fog and observe as objectively as possible. *Does this feel true to my purpose, my goals and dreams? Where do I need clarity to remove, distill, and continue?*

REVERSED: Are you feeling overwhelmed by choices right now? Step back and, rather than examining what's in front of you, think about what you want from this situation. Be honest and compassionate with yourself as you consider why overwhelm is coming up to the surface.

IMAGINED MENTORS

Who do you envision when you think of someone who's really got this whole life thing down? Imagine that person being met with the challenge you're facing and how they might interact with it. Go deeper by meditating and having an imaginary conversation with them. What can you gain from interviewing the part of yourself you see as wise, accomplished, and capable?

EIGHT OF CUPS

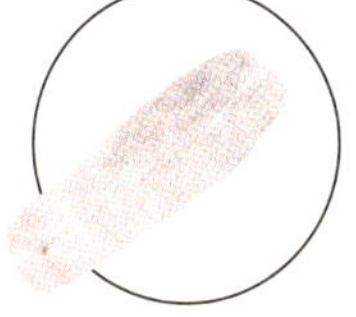

GEM

Kunzite
TENDER LOVING CARE, CUDDLES, LOVE

SONG

"Dancing On My Own"
ROBYN

SCENT

CRUMPLED TISSUE AND SALT

It's hard to see all our efforts laid before us and realize it simply isn't enough to remain invested. You've put in the work. *And yet . . .* this card is a clear and resounding call to move on. If you're stuck in an emotionally sticky situation, it's going to be a lot to walk away from, but you have given everything you've got. It's painful and scary to give up, but bravery isn't a lack of fear; it's being afraid and forging ahead anyway.

REVERSED: When we're facing heartbreak, grief, or any substantial emotional challenge, it can be easy to think that life will keep disappointing us. All good things must come to an end, but we often ignore the obvious inverse: Every bad streak ends, too. Each bad cycle is punctuated with good. If you find yourself thinking the good never lasts, just remember, neither does the bad.

EMBRACING SUFFERING

There is simply no existence without pain. If we label the experience of pain as just one expression of life itself, then we can neutralize it. Try to imagine that emotional suffering is the universe (or whatever god you might worship) embracing your humanity and providing you with a new opportunity to experience being alive. Joy is not "good" and grief is not "bad," they simply exist.

NINE OF CUPS

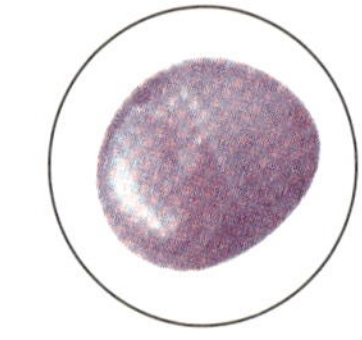

GEM

Amethyst
SPIRITUAL WISDOM, HUMILITY, PROTECTION

SONG

"Thank You"
BONNIE RAITT

SCENT

YOUR BEST FRIEND'S EMBRACE

There's a lot to luxuriate in right now! You've worked hard for what you have, and you deserve to soak up the abundance. Surround yourself with treasures and bask in the incredible life you've created. Your bright inner light is radiating, attracting goodness and prosperity, and the more you embrace your wealth of mind, body, and soul, the more you'll find to appreciate. Gratitude is a high-yield investment.

REVERSED: You may be feeling under-enthused about your current circumstance, *or* you might be feeling greedy. Listen, we live in an exhausting, challenging world, and resources are precious! Whatever you do have in abundance, though, you have a lot of it. You can manifest more joy and abundance by reflecting on what you appreciate—*and* by sharing the wealth where it makes sense.

MANIFESTATION

In a journal, identify your greatest wish and create concrete steps to make it come true. You have the power, the resources, and the mindset to make it all come together. Don't hold back! How might you strengthen the spell you've cast? What metaphorical drops can be added to your bucket? Keep building on what you've already accomplished and you will inevitably go far.

TEN OF CUPS

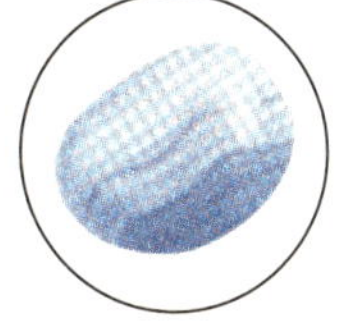

GEM

Blue lace agate
OPEN HEART,
EMOTIONAL STRENGTH,
UNCONDITIONAL LOVE

SONG

"Mango Pops"
ELLE MÚSA

SCENT

BUTTERCREAM
FROSTING

The Ten of Cups symbolizes ultimate emotional achievement. Your deepest desires have come to fruition. Feel it fully. Soak in the emotional fulfillment in your life. Your community is abundant; your support system is here. There's opportunity to look forward to, and loads of love in the present. Celebrate all that you have worked hard to create!

REVERSED: Your ideal emotional landscape may feel far away right now. Reflect on what parts of your life you haven't been enjoying. Take a few steps back and review the Eight and Nine of Cups. How are your heart's investments panning out? Consider what you want from your Ten of Cups.

TEN CUPS OF GRATITUDE

Put ten pieces of paper out in front of you. Label each of these "cups" with one of the ten most important sections of your life (we might suggest mind, body, heart, spirit, home, family, career, hobbies, inspiration, and goals, but you can customize your vessels as you see fit). Write down things you're grateful for in each category (it might be a good idea to set a timer for each section). Combine your papers into a booklet of reminders of all you have to appreciate in your life. Review it when you aren't feeling super sparkly.

APPRENTICE OF CUPS

GEM

Seraphinite
EMOTIONAL DEVELOPMENT, CONNECTIVITY, INNER STRENGTH

SONG

"Dreams"
THE CRANBERRIES

SCENT

STARGAZER LILIES

This sweet baby is here to help usher in a new season of learning about your emotions. Don't worry—this is a gentle beginning! The Apprentice of Cups is learning about their deepest feelings. Maybe you're experiencing a crush or falling in love with the world, discovering new parts of yourself you're especially proud of . . . whatever beautiful connections you're making, welcome them. There are infinite treasures to uncover!

REVERSED: Are you feeling a creative or emotional block right now? There's something to be said for curiosity. Ask some questions instead of meeting your struggle with frustration. Think of this conversation as one you might have with your inner child. Be gentle and honest with yourself; honor this vulnerability.

Imagine the Apprentice of Cups and the Fool as best friends. Describe the perfect friend date between these two cards—and then do your best to re-create it, either solo or with a real-life loved one!

DREAM DATE

CHAMPION OF CUPS

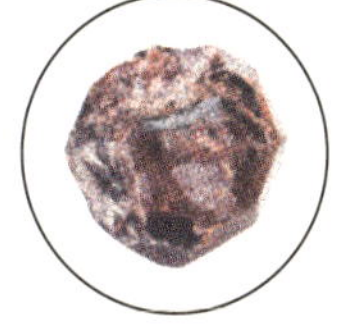

GEM

Garnet
CREATION, ARTISTRY, AROUSAL

SONG

"Someone New"
HOZIER

SCENT

A BOX OF ARTISANAL CHOCOLATES

The Champion of Cups is the artist of the tarot. A true poet, speaking truth through abstract and creative means, their sensuality and vulnerability drive their work. They may appear secretive, withdrawn, eternally youthful. Their energy may trigger self-judgment or strike envy from observers. This is not your problem to solve. The Champion's sensitive nature makes it easy for others to pick and prod. But it is in this sensitive space that they hold ultimate power, a knowing of self that others envy.

REVERSED: Romantic energy can be the juice that ignites passion in your work and personal life, but it can also disconnect you from reality. Take a moment for a reality check. Where are emotions getting ahead of you? A dose of practicality (even something dull and methodical) could do you some good right now.

AROUSAL OF THE SENSES

Our senses are our primary tools for observing life at large. Note a few things that activate each of your senses and reference this list when your senses need awakening.

ORACLE OF CUPS

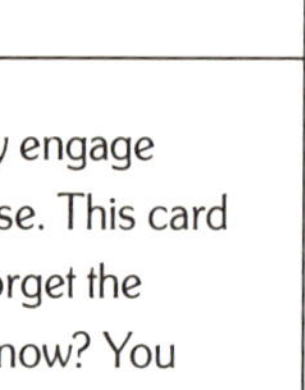

The Oracle sits on their throne aware of their feelings, how they engage with the world, and the pure divinity of every atom in the universe. This card represents a grounded inner knowing and asks the reader to forget the head and trust the gut. What do you *feel* is the right thing, right now? You may try to justify things with logic, but now is the time to rule wisely with the insight you've gained as an emotional being.

REVERSED: It's time to take a break from being everyone's strongest support beam; it's beginning to wear on you. When we focus too much on what we have to offer our community, we forget to take care of ourselves. Self-respect is holy. Do not work so hard that you begin to resent those around you. Beware of codependency.

GEM

Astrophyllite
PSYCHIC POWER, INSIGHT, FEMININE STRENGTH

SONG

"Les Fleurs"
MINNIE RIPERTON

SCENT

A BUBBLE BATH FILLED WITH ROSE PETALS AND LUXURIOUS OILS

BOUNDARIES AS SELF, SELF AS HOME

Boundaries are fences around the house of our soul. We have the right to decide who we let in and how much of our space they take up, and we get to uphold the rules of our "house." Inside is where those closest to you may roam. Outside, you have a big yard to host friends, family, and neighbors. This is a space where people you want to spend time with—but maybe don't trust to come into your home—can be found.

You are your home. In the illustration here, write out the boundaries you uphold within yourself (the house), which ones you have in place in your life (the yard), and what boundaries help you let people in (the stone path).

ELDER OF CUPS

GEM

Ruby
PASSION, SEXUAL PROWESS, INTENSE PROTECTION

SONG

"girl from sedna"
LOU VAL & VAUGHN

SCENT

A WELL-LOVED LEATHER JOURNAL

The master of the suit of emotions knows how to commune with the inner workings of relationships and their outward-reaching roots. Embrace a holistic view of the emotional world. Hold its positives and negatives in neutralizing hands and know there is no "bad" feeling—there is only *feeling*. This deep, emotional knowing makes it easy to turn life lessons into creative expression. Tap into the Elder of Cups to make your next masterpiece, or simply to express your innermost yearnings. Dig deep. You can handle it.

REVERSED: Mastery of emotions is one thing. Manipulation is another. The situation at hand requires maturity, or perhaps someone is hiding ulterior motives. Remember: We can only be as honest with others as we are with ourselves. Is everyone involved in your current situation able to be honest with themselves?

TRANSMUTING EMOTIONS INTO ART

List the colors, scents, songs, textures, synonyms, and/or any other associations that come to mind when you think of the emotions listed below. Next time you're struggling to express yourself while experiencing any of these feelings, consult the associations you've named here and see if they help to put words to your experience.

LOVE

GRIEF

ANGER

JOY

INSECURITY

PRIDE

Swords

ELEMENTAL CONNECTION: Air
EMBODIMENT: Our Intellect and Reasoning

The Swords slice to the bone, revealing our cerebral selves. This is the suit of ideas, theory, and philosophy. The air signs Gemini, Libra, and Aquarius will likely see a lot of themselves within these cards. Many concepts depicted by the Swords are challenging, but on the other side of these experiences comes relief, and room for expansion and growth. What is greater than the feeling of overcoming a natural obstacle? The sense of self-worth and healthy pride gained makes the hurdle worth the jump. We encourage you to read the Swords with an open mind so that you may harvest the lessons fully rather than fear the obstacles inherent to living one's life.

CONCEPTS TO EXPLORE WITH THE SUIT OF SWORDS:

- ○ *Gliding through challenges with grace*
- ○ *Magic and mystery in the unseen*
- ○ *Giving others their air space*
- ○ *Thoughts in our orbit*

CONNECT WITH SWORDS:
Slow down, distract your mind, and release stress with box breathing. Breathe out slowly, releasing all the air from your lungs. Breathe in through your nose for four counts. Hold your breath for four counts, exhale for four counts, hold again for four counts, and then release. Repeat this process three more times and you'll find yourself breathing deeper and slower, with a calmer spirit and a centered mind.

LIST YOUR THOUGHTS

Gazing into the cards in the Swords suit, what thoughts do you have? In the spaces below, write out the first things that come to mind when seeing the reflections, blades, and powerful animals depicted on the cards. Perhaps the ant in the mighty Apprentice reminds you that you need to take out the trash, or the puffin in the Six of Swords stirs up memories of a trip to see those beautiful birds in the flesh. Allow thoughts to pour onto the page, no matter how mundane or silly they might be. Create this list again after several months of regular tarot practice.

ACE: ___

TWO: ___

THREE: ___

FOUR: ___

FIVE: ___

SIX: ___

SEVEN: ___

EIGHT: ___

NINE: ___

TEN: ___

APPRENTICE: ___

CHAMPION: ___

ORACLE: ___

ELDER: ___

TAKE IT FURTHER

Using the list of thoughts above, journal about what might be lying underneath the impulse of your initial observations. Are there any themes? Strengthen your intuition by learning to appreciate the first thought and its more deeply attached roots simultaneously. So, take the trash out if the cards remind you to, but also ask yourself: *What's beyond the action?*

ACE OF SWORDS

GEM

Diamond
CLARITY, STRENGTH, PERSEVERANCE

SONG

"I Can See Clearly Now"
JOHNNY NASH

SCENT

BASIL AND CILANTRO

This singular sword brings with it a bittersweet energy that colors the entire suit. You are on the first leg of a new journey, and though it is headed in a beautiful direction, moving forward will also come with loss. Perhaps the loss is something cerebral, like an old way of thinking or a belief system, but maybe it was more tangible: a precious item, a sacred place, or an important person. Whatever you've moved on from, know that the grief you feel in this new phase of life does not undo the gratitude you feel. Letting go of what no longer serves you . . . *serves you.*

REVERSED: Are you hanging on to something that no longer works just because change is scary? You're holding yourself back. When the time comes to cut away the excess and you refuse, you are turning your sword against yourself. Be your own hero: Turn the sword outward, not inward.

HONORING GRIEF

Write a letter of gratitude for your grief. What can you find inside your grief that will help you become the best version of yourself? What does your grief have to teach you? Explore your feelings with this letter. Don't be afraid to forge on. You've got your sword and your wisdom. You can do this.

TWO OF SWORDS

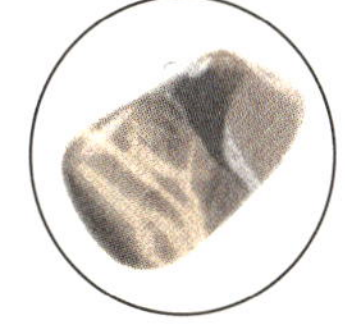

GEM

Tiger's eye
CLAIRVOYANCE, MOOD BALANCING, MEDITATION

SONG

"Motion Sickness"
PHOEBE BRIDGERS

SCENT

STALE AIR IN A MUSTY ROOM

It's decision time and you're feeling avoidant. Where in your current life do you feel like there are two opposing forces keeping you from moving forward? Close your eyes with intention to find your grounding inner voice. You might sleep late and zone out these days. Remember: Only close your eyes when it feels grounding, not avoidant, as life is still moving forward. Making no choice will leave you in an unending state of anxiety. Eradicate fear and make your choice, knowing nothing is perfect.

REVERSED: You may find yourself feeling stuck by choosing to be a peacemaker, the mediator in a conflict. Your intentions to bring people together are good, but once you become the emotional dumping ground for those around you, it's time to remove yourself.

WEIGH YOUR PROS AND CONS

When you feel you must choose between two paths, use this simple tarot spread to explore each option. On your left, pull a card representing Choice A and a second representing its impact on you. On the right, repeat this for Choice B.

Use a journal to reflect. Repeat this spread whenever you need help in future decision making.

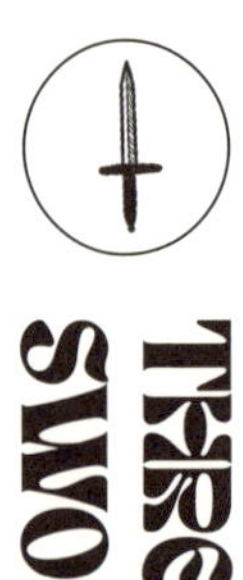

THREE OF SWORDS

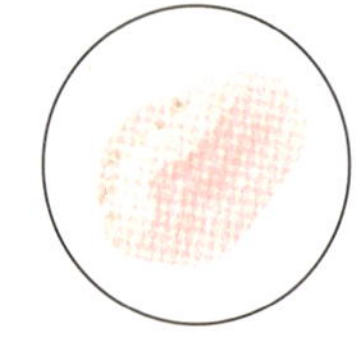

GEM

Rhodochrosite
GENTLENESS,
HEARTBREAK SUPPORT,
HEALING GRIEF

SONG

"Add Value Add Time"
SHILPA RAY

SCENT

WELL-WORN CLOTHES

Ouch! Your heart hurts and for a valid reason. Entanglement and confusion are making a romantic relationship (be it platonic or sexual) messy as hell. Now is the time to have a good cry. . . . Release it all, baby. This pain is temporary. On your own, you are destined to discover a renewed sense of self. Heartbreak and loss like this help you see more clearly what you deserve and what you will and will not stand for. Peace and stillness are just one step away. Growth is happening.

REVERSED: Are you speaking negatively to yourself? Cut it out! Speak to yourself like you're speaking to a sweet little kiddo. We all hold an inner child who needs nurturing. Be your own parent. Practice speaking to yourself and others with gentleness.

THREE CARDS FOR CLARITY

If you find yourself questioning your own perception and you pull this card? The Three of Swords says it's not you; it's them. Clear the confusion with this spread.

FIRST CARD	SECOND CARD	THIRD CARD
What to leave behind	*What to take with you*	*What you need to know to find a fresh start*

FOUR OF SWORDS

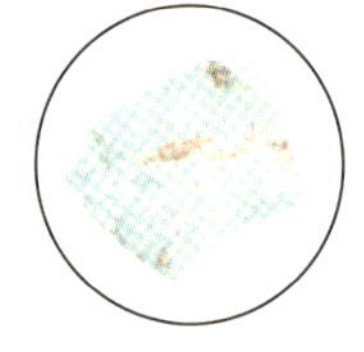

GEM

Chrysoprase
FORGIVENESS, COMFORT, RELEASING TEARS

SONG

"Sick of Losing Soulmates"
DODIE

SCENT

HOT CHOCOLATE WITH NUTMEG

Consider the fours as solid structures. The challenge presented here is to find stillness despite looming fear or worry. Perhaps you've recently experienced tension and trauma within a relationship, or had financial or health worries, or maybe persistent stress has been poking at you for some time now. You need a moment of retreat. You are a separate being from the stress that nips at your ankles. Time in stillness is what's needed right now. Focus on releasing shame around sticky situations that have drained you. Give yourself a hug, get cozy, and take a break before moving forward.

REVERSED: This reversal is a gentle nudge to consider where you're busying yourself for no other reason than distraction. Take a moment to assess where you're spinning your wheels without any movement forward. Be honest with yourself.

Feel first, think later! When we're struggling to feel safety and calm, it's easy to become detached from our bodies. Using a "bottom up" strategy (meaning addressing physical needs before mental ones) can help us regulate in these moments. Use this exercise to carve out some much-needed rest and recuperation—whether or not you can take a full-on vacation.

MAKE A LIST OF EVERY NON-TECHNOLOGICAL SOURCE OF COMFORT YOU CAN THINK OF FROM YOUR PAST AND PRESENT:

This coming weekend, set aside a few hours to delight in as many of these comforts as you can. Indulge in softness.

FIVE OF SWORDS

The cycle of life promises that every ending is the dawn of a beginning—for each low there is a high. While this reminder may feel buoyant in the seas of despair, it's important to note that how you feel and what is happening *now* are important. No buoy can take away the pain you might be experiencing, and sometimes the most healing thing of all can be to accept defeat, witness loss, and just sit with the pain. It's okay to feel soaked to the bone in the cold for now. Don't wallow; simply experience it.

REVERSED: You've been fighting hard to make something work that just isn't a possibility. Ouuuuch . . . your ego is feeling wounded by that truth. Trust that the vulnerability you'll feel from stopping your fight is what will move you forward.

Color in the scales of this snake. With each scale, imagine yourself actively renewing yourself, growing new shining scales of armor to bolster the strength that already lies within you.

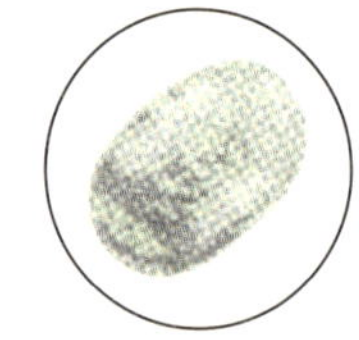

GEM

Serpentine
REPTILIAN RENEWAL, CIRCULATION, RECOUPING

SONG

"Stay Soft"
MITSKI

SCENT

SEAWEED AND FRESH OCEAN WAVES

REPTILIAN RENEWAL

SIX OF SWORDS

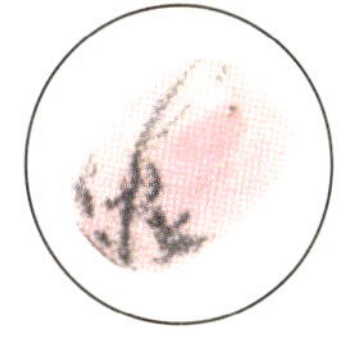

GEM

Rhodonite
HOPE, MOVEMENT, REVITALIZATION

SONG

"Be Sweet"
JAPANESE BREAKFAST

SCENT

CRISP PINEAPPLE SLICES AND CRUSHED MINT

Change is the name of the game right now, and with change comes boundary work. The past may have been turbulent, and you carry the scars of those battles with you for some time, but the road ahead looks clear. You're moving on. Some days may be confusing, and you might find yourself wondering if you've made the right decision. Remind yourself that with life comes pain—and so we should choose the painless route as often as we can. Living shouldn't be so very hard when it doesn't have to be.

REVERSED: You're holding off on making a difficult choice to leave a situation that is not in your favor. Sometimes it's helpful to ask why you're struggling to move on. Other times it's helpful to make the leap and assess later, from the safety of someplace new. Consider which path may be best for you—the one you're on isn't doing you any good.

YOUR PRIZED POSSESSIONS

In a journal, try these prompts:

1. If you were able to save just three things from your home before it all vanished, what would you choose?
2. If you were able to save just three things within yourself, what would you choose?
3. What does this reflect, and what can you release?

SEVEN OF SWORDS

In the traditional depiction of this card, a figure carries five swords, looking over their shoulder at two they've left behind. Perhaps they're watching their back as they steal someone else's swords, or they might be trying to direct the viewer's attention to something other than their own theft. Consider who is showing you what they want you to see right now. Or if you find yourself being deceitful, this card might be telling you that you're not being as slick as you thought.

REVERSED: It's possible to give too much. Are you the one who's always giving out great advice, showing up with more food to put on the table, and giving so much from your own pocket that you can't afford your rent? Consider some boundary work, friend. You aren't being honest with yourself about how much you have to give.

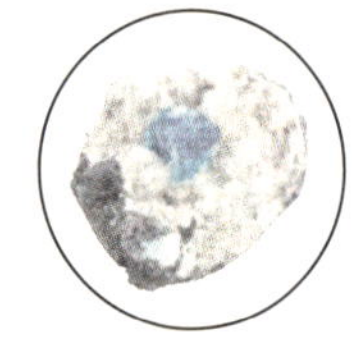

GEM

Cavansite
TRUTH, HONESTY, SPEAKING, WRITING

SONG

"Secrets and Lies"
RUELLE

SCENT

MOTHBALLS

DO YOU BELIEVE YOUR BOUNDARIES ARE . . .

○ **TOO SOFT** ○ **MALLEABLE** ○ **FIRM** ○ **TOO RIGID**

Journal prompt: What can you do to create more balance? What is one new way to continue the work you've been doing?

BOLDENING BOUNDARIES

EIGHT OF SWORDS

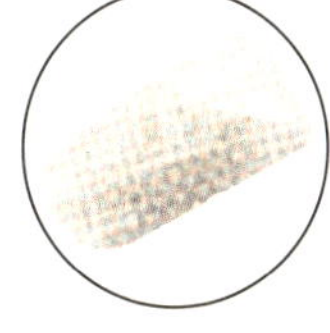

GEM

Danburite
ELEVATED THINKING, BUZZING ENERGY, SPARKS

SONG

"Trapped in My Mind"
KID CUDI

SCENT

CACTUS BLOSSOM AND SAND

In what areas of your life do you feel ignorant to what's right in front of you? Limiting beliefs are telling you that the situation you are currently in is out of your control. But the truth is, you can claim freedom for yourself. Wake up to your self-imposed restrictions. Sure, there are blades surrounding you—they may even appear immovable. But you are strong. Pull away one of the swords being held against you (you are, after all, the one holding it), toss it to the side, and take a step forward.

REVERSED: You're releasing yourself from the negative thought patterns and belief systems of your past. They were never yours to begin with. As you shed these old narratives, know that the true you will be revealed more and more as you continue on your path.

CHALLENGING FALSE BOUNDARIES

Worry exists with reason. This week, allow yourself a daily five-minute session of listing out all the things weighing you down. Thoughts are powerful, but when we acknowledge them, we can shape them. Evaluate what comes up this week and how you might want to adjust in both action and outlook. What's true and what narratives feel false? At the end of the week, remember: You are the author of your life. Edit accordingly.

NINE OF SWORDS

This is your prompt to check in on your cycling negative thoughts. Fears and worries can turn into self-fulfilling prophecies if you don't stop and check in. Manifestation is a powerful tool, and you have the choice right now to either continue manifesting your fears into realities (what a waste of your time!) or focus on goals that bring you joy, comfort, and hope. Enlist the help of others. Stay accountable as you move in a more positive direction. You deserve the support.

REVERSED: You've been in a situation that has caused you to freak out in fear. Pause and realize how far you've come already; the worst has already passed. It's up to you to reset to a headspace of hopefulness. There are good things to come. Shed the past and let it remain there.

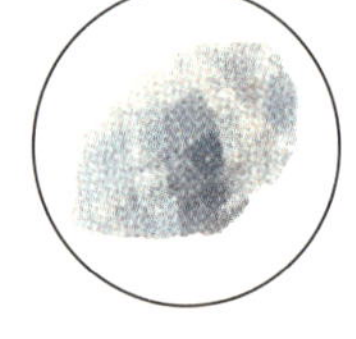

GEM

Blue calcite
STRESS RELIEF, GENTLE ENERGY, CALM

SONG

"Uninvited"
ALANIS MORISSETTE

SCENT

SANDALWOOD AND CEDAR

TEMPERATURE REGULATION

Try this grounding practice to help you return to center when you feel activated by fear: Regulate your emotions by re-regulating your body's temperature.

Place ice packs on your feet or your face for a couple minutes at a time, or run a hot bath and give yourself a good lavender body scrub (a texture change like a scrub can regulate you, too). Feel your emotions shift as you experience a sensation shift.

IN THE LINES BELOW, LIST OUT DIFFERENT WAYS THAT YOU CAN CREATE A CHANGE IN YOUR ENVIRONMENT TO SPARK A SHIFT IN YOUR MOOD.

TEN OF SWORDS

This card could easily be called "the dark night of the soul." An unexpected ending—perhaps a betrayal or devastating failure—has shocked your system and left a deep ache. It's a reality check that feels crushing, but there is at least one gift to be found here. The silver lining that's hiding in this moment is very real. So are you. Even a boulder that weighs a thousand pounds can be moved with enough strength. Don't forget that many hands make light work. The loving forces in your life can help lighten this load.

REVERSED: Being haunted by past pain can be a terribly sticky thing. Keep walking with it and, like with something stuck to your shoe, you may just get it all over everything. The best thing to do is take the time to clean up the mess sooner rather than later.

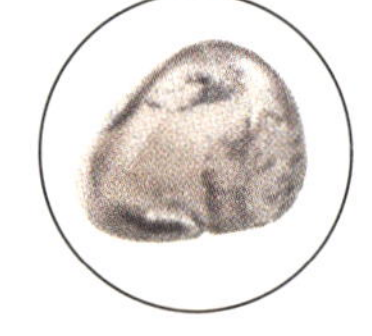

GEM

Smoky quartz
DRAMA DEFLECTION, CENTERING, PROTECTION

SONG

"The First Cut Is the Deepest"
P. P. ARNOLD

SCENT

A MUD PUDDLE

Trusting your inner knowledge can be a hard task. This exercise will help you develop a sense of embodied truth.

LIST TEN UNDENIABLE TRUTHS BELOW—ANYTHING FROM "WHITE WINE GETS OUT RED WINE" TO "I AM WORTHY OF LOVE."

THE SWAY TEST: Every morning for a week, stand tall with your arms engaged and palms facing forward. Say something you know to be true and notice how your body lightly leans forward. Now say something absurdly untrue and feel your body pull back. Your intuition guides you, leaning forward in truth and pulling back when something feels wrong. Practice this, speaking truths and untruths each morning this week to cultivate your self-trust.

APPRENTICE OF SWORDS

Honest, insightful, and frank, the Apprentice of Swords embodies a feminine energy whose strength is found in clear communication and an openness to new ideas. Take this as a sign to be bold in your personal expression. Look out for opportunities—stay curious and alert. Why not take a risk? Try public speaking, start a blog or podcast, or initiate conversations with people you find intimidating. Think of it as an exploration phase, a time to be bold. Because isn't that what all of life is, anyway?

REVERSED: Always be prepared for things to go off-track. That doesn't mean you should hold back on acting out your plans—you should always be moving in the direction of your dreams! This reversal simply asks you to remain aware.

GEM

Blue tiger's eye
ENLIGHTENMENT, REVOLUTION, METAMORPHOSIS

SONG

"Hunter"
BECCA MANCARI

SCENT

BUBBLY SHAMPOO

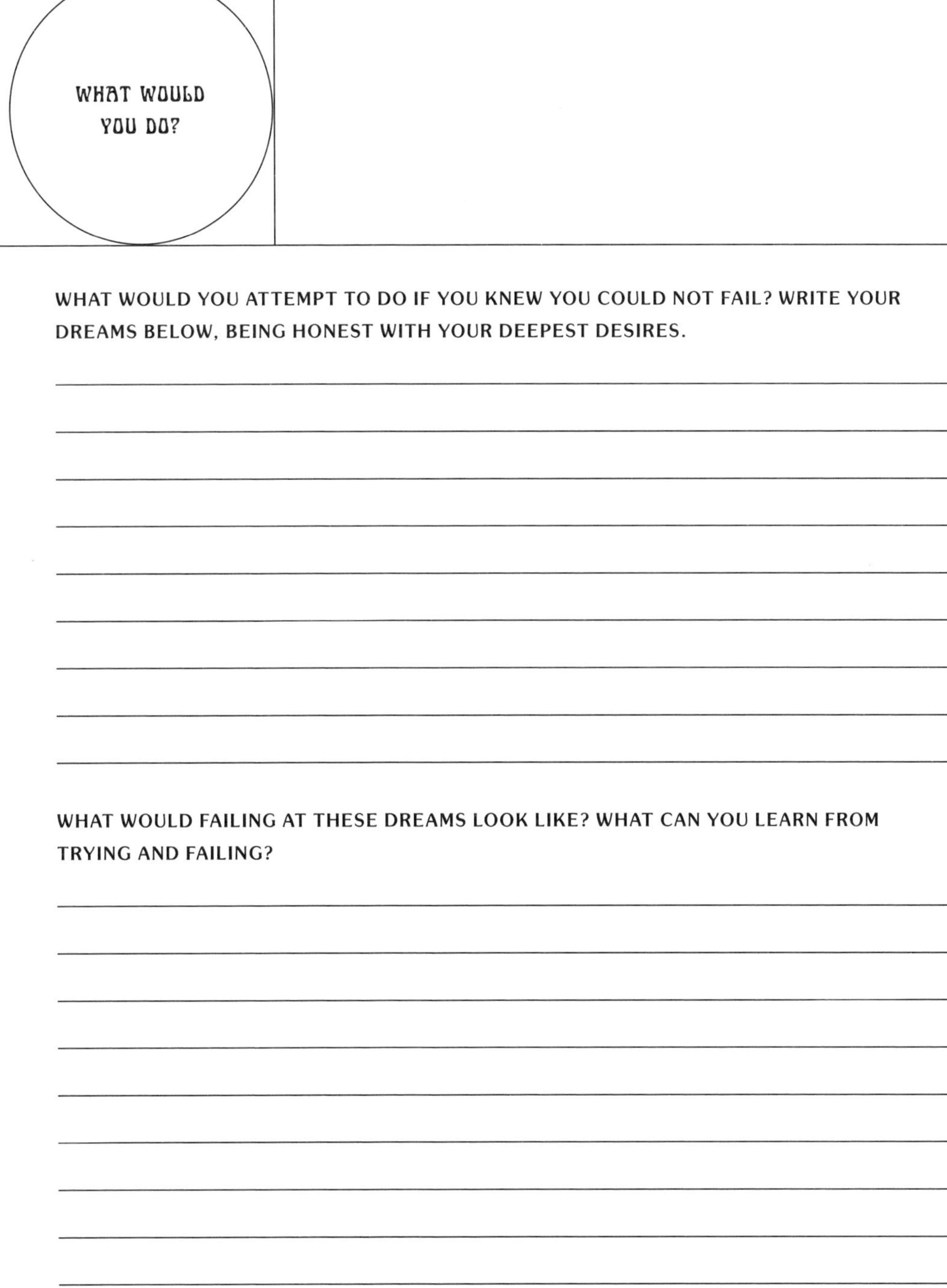

WHAT WOULD YOU ATTEMPT TO DO IF YOU KNEW YOU COULD NOT FAIL? WRITE YOUR DREAMS BELOW, BEING HONEST WITH YOUR DEEPEST DESIRES.

WHAT WOULD FAILING AT THESE DREAMS LOOK LIKE? WHAT CAN YOU LEARN FROM TRYING AND FAILING?

CHAMPION OF SWORDS

The parts of us that can be seen in all our colorful, outward flourishes are so different than what's at our core, beyond the tree line, deep down in our souls. The Champion of Swords struts into your world today to remind you that you cannot just walk the walk, but you must also allow yourself stillness; *feel* into the path you're on, regardless of the distractions in the forest of life. Stay true to your core as you wander down the trail ahead. Be thoughtful about the endeavors you commit to. Check in often. Breathe deeply. Persevere.

REVERSED: You may be approaching certain issues in your life with unchecked power imbalances, aggression, or even tyranny. Look at what's going on when you encounter triggers and interrogate the motivation behind your frustrations. What's really pecking at you? Whatever it is, you're tempted to misplace your upset. Don't.

GEM

Bismuth
TRANSITION ASSISTANCE, VIGOR, PROGRESS

SONG

"9 to 5"
DOLLY PARTON

SCENT

FRESHLY CRACKED PEPPER

GEM

Black tourmaline
BOUNDARIES, ANALYTICAL OBSERVATION, RESPECT

SONG

"Catalog of Unabashed Gratitude"
ROSS GAY WITH BON IVER

SCENT

CANDLELIGHT AND A BAMBOO RAINFOREST

The Elder of Swords can be viewed as the sun. Without it life would cease, but it is dangerous, too. They are the keeper of the flame, the fire of the belly, the match from which all life burns bright. Consider each side of the Elder's blade and how an object used for defense and safety can be misused as a weapon to cut others down. Be aware of the power in your life. It requires a delicate balance. Here, trust has been well earned.

REVERSED: Corruption can get the best of us, as the view from the top can become clouded and spoiled. Investigate your allies and your use of power carefully.

PERCEPTION VS. REALITY

What are some misconceptions others have about you? Journal about the most potent point of contention you experience. Interrogate this perception. Use three full pages to explore why and how others might misunderstand you, what's informing their opinion, and end with a list of those who understand you BEST in this way. List the ways they support you in your truth, then use this to help clarify who's on your team—and how that looks in action.

Pentacles

ELEMENTAL CONNECTION: Earth
EMBODIMENT: Our Outward Behavior and Actions

The suit of Pentacles drops into our readings with an abundance of wisdom regarding our human existence. This is the suit of Earth, where Taurus, Virgo, and Capricorn are at home. The Pentacles—also known as Coins—are often related to attainment, wealth, home, and hearth. When viewed through the lens of mental health, Pentacles symbolize our outward behaviors. They can also represent strife and struggle. It's important to remember that all physical attachments come and go. Read these cards with the knowledge that there is nothing purely positive or negative within the tarot: All is subjective. Consider how every precious suit of the tarot informs your outward behavior.

CONNECT WITH PENTACLES:
Stand barefoot on the ground. Visualize roots growing from the bottom of your feet, connecting with the earth. Extend your arms out, imagining leaves and branches growing out from the trunk of your body. Close your eyes and picture the sun beaming down on your growing limbs, warming every inch of your being. Breathe in deep, trusting that you are connected to the earth and glowing under the light of the sun.

CONCEPTS TO EXPLORE WITH THE SUIT OF PENTACLES:

- ○ *What behavior of yours is learned, as opposed to inherent*
- ○ *How to get grounded*
- ○ *The roots of being*
- ○ *Connecting with nature*

LIST YOUR VALUES

Look over the images in the suit of Pentacles and see what connections you can make between the cards and your earthly existence. When you see these objects—the piggy bank, the broken vase, the old coins, the animals—what can you tie them to in your own life? The broken vase in the Five of Pentacles may remind you of an urn above your mantel, or a bouquet of flowers. If a connection exists in your mind, it's worth noting here. Try to relate each card to a solid object, person, or place in your life and list it here.

ACE: __________

TWO: __________

THREE: __________

FOUR: __________

FIVE: __________

SIX: __________

SEVEN: __________

EIGHT: __________

NINE: __________

TEN: __________

APPRENTICE: __________

CHAMPION: __________

ORACLE: __________

ELDER: __________

TAKE IT FURTHER

What do these people, places, and things mean to you? Journal about what each of these connections carries for you on an emotional level. By looking beyond the surface of our theoretical and physical associations and into the heart behind them, we're able to understand our intuitive connection to each card. So if a broken vase reminds you of an urn, that probably has a lot of complex emotion behind it. Write about this. Allow yourself to sit with your conscious and subconscious connections.

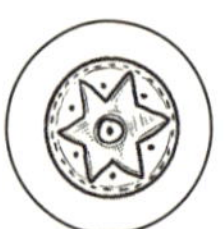

ACE OF PENTACLES

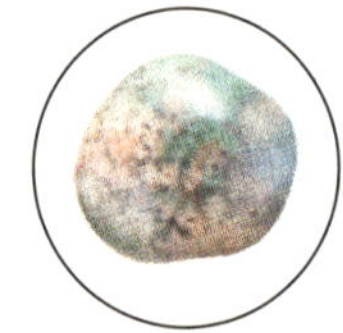

GEM

Moss agate
TRANQUILITY, STABILITY, ELIMINATION OF NEGATIVITY

SONG

"Money"
THE FLYING LIZARDS

SCENT

CRISP CASH AND SPARKLING COINS

You are being presented with a unique path forward in pursuit of life's stability. Perhaps a career opportunity or a financial boon has appeared, or maybe you're seeking something new. This is your sign to start fresh. Go forth and take a chance on yourself! This card indicates that your investments of time, energy, and money are well-placed, and you can count on yourself to follow through.

REVERSED: You might be overlooking an opportunity that would serve you well. Now is the time to examine your fears around stability. Which worries keep you safe and which are holding you back from what you truly deserve? Alternately, keep an eye on your investments and know when to move on.

CREATE YOUR ALTAR

Your altar is the place where you can do anything from sitting in contemplation to meditating, manifesting, or practicing your personal form of spirituality. Anyone can create an altar in their home, workspace, or even vehicle. This space is yours, but we have a few suggestions for getting started if you aren't sure where to begin.

- ◯ Choose a space away from electronics as your altar space. Turn off your phone when you are near it to help protect the natural energy you cultivate.
- ◯ Add crystals, candles, lucky charms, objects of significance, incense, flowers, or pictures of deities, heroes, and those you love.
- ◯ Add elements to represent the five points of the pentacle:
    - ◯ **NORTH/EARTH:** *A bowl of salt or sand*
    - ◯ **EAST/AIR:** *A feather or the smoke from incense*
    - ◯ **WEST/WATER:** *Moon water (see page 67) or clear quartz in water*
    - ◯ **SOUTH/FIRE:** *A candle*
    - ◯ **THE FIFTH POINT/THE SPIRIT:** *A photo of an ancestor or deity*

Take five minutes each day this week to sit at your altar as a part of your morning or evening ritual. If you aren't sure what to do here, try simply sipping a cup of tea and looking at all the beautiful objects you've gathered. Practice being present.

DID YOU KNOW THE *EVERY LITTLE THING YOU DO IS MAGIC TAROT DECK* MAKES THE PERFECT MINI ALTAR? USE ITS INCLUDED CARD STAND TO DISPLAY YOUR TAROT CARD OF THE DAY AND ASSEMBLE YOUR CHOSEN OBJECTS AROUND IT TO CREATE YOUR SACRED SPACE.

TWO OF PENTACLES

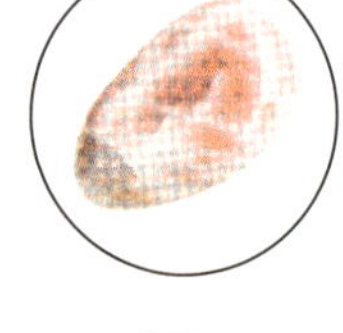

GEM

Moonstone
VULNERABILITY, PRIORITIZATION, FRAGILITY

SONG

"Be Here Now"
RAY LAMONTAGNE

SCENT

RAIN-SOAKED SOIL

There's a lot happening in your material life, whether in terms of your homestead, career, or finances. "A lot" does not necessarily mean "too much," though. Bring your attention to how you frame things. Are you saying you don't have time for things when you're not *making* time? If so, consider your priorities—maybe those things you're "too busy" for aren't at the top of your list, and that's okay! You're doing a great job balancing things. Cut yourself some slack. You're juggling it all with grace.

REVERSED: You might be ignoring your priorities in favor of what might make others happy. Your imbalance is beginning to have a negative impact in your life. Time to make some changes and figure out what's most important to tend to. Reprioritize your happiness before others'.

Assess the balance of things in your material life. How heavy do each of these things feel? Mark where you are on the spectrum of light to heavy.

WORK	LIGHT	HEAVY
HOME	LIGHT	HEAVY
COMMUNITY	LIGHT	HEAVY
ROMANCE	LIGHT	HEAVY
FINANCE	LIGHT	HEAVY

WHAT ARE SOME WAYS TO CREATE MORE LIGHTNESS IN AREAS THAT FEEL TOO HEAVY?

THREE OF PENTACLES

GEM

Peridot
SUCCESS, MONEY, MAGNETIC ENERGY

SONG

"Everything You Touch Is Gold"
GREGORY PORTER

SCENT

BUBBLY CHAMPAGNE

Your collaborations—with friends, coworkers, lovers, etc.—are aligned in a truly divine way. There's something special going on in the connections you have, and it's supporting your wellness in a holistic way. Perhaps the most beautiful thing happening is that each person or element at play brings their own unique qualities (and flaws!) to the table. When we're honest about what we have capacity for and others do the same, we can be valuable to one another without abandoning ourselves.

REVERSED: Maximize your ability to create abundance by collaborating with your community. Nobody does it alone! When we can find common ground with those around us, we achieve a kind of alignment that infuses our collaborative work with magic. It's time to be vulnerable about your own weaknesses so that your community has the chance to support you!

Identify a moment when you were supported in a meaningful way. How have you grown since then? In what ways are you richer now? Journal about this experience and how it's added value to your life today. Next, brainstorm about how to pay that support forward. Donations, volunteering, or helping someone directly can all honor both your past self and the person who helped you.

PAYING SUPPORT FORWARD

FOUR OF PENTACLES

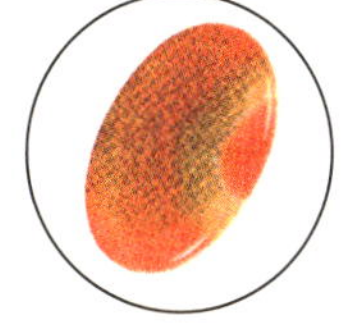

GEM

Fire agate
ASSISTANCE, EMBODIMENT, SHIELDING

SONG

"I Don't Really Care for You"
CMAT

SCENT

IRON AND STEEL

The pursuit of stability and a quality life is a healthy one, but unfortunately it can distort into greed, selfishness, and a scarcity mindset. Your financial and physical goals are worthwhile, but be wary of spending too much time (or money) by yourself. You might feel alone in your endeavors—maybe you're the breadwinner of the family, or maybe you're a breaker of intergenerational trauma around finances—and you need to be surrounded by supportive, loving hands. How can you get more trustworthy, solid people on your team?

REVERSED: Check in on your current spending habits. Are you overspending? Feeling a bit greedy, perhaps? If it's not money you're indulging in, how else are you retreating, hiding, and hoarding your time, energy, and gifts? It's likely a response to trauma. Don't close off. Keep yourself open in spite of the trauma.

ACTS OF INVESTMENT AND PROTECTION

We often seek out protectors in the form of others when what we need most is to cultivate protection from within.

In a journal, write down something within yourself that you believe deserves protection, then ask yourself: *What's one thing you can do to defend this aspect of self? What can prevent harm from befalling this aspect? And how can you strengthen and empower this part of yourself?*

FIVE OF PENTACLES

GEM

Bloodstone
RESTORATION, REDIRECTION, MOTIVATION

SONG

"You Can't Always Get What You Want"
RUSTED ROOT

SCENT

CRISP, ICY AIR

Times are tough. This card is known to pop up when bank accounts and cupboards are empty, when we're mourning an earth-shattering breakup, or when we're fresh out of hope for a better future. The bad news? Fives are often painful. The good news? They're halfway through the cycle of ten. You're on your way out! For now, consider how you feel and let it wash over you like a tide. Allow it to come, allow it to pass. Six, seven, and beyond are waiting for you once the ocean of grief dries up.

REVERSED: You're on the mend after a period of financial struggle. Or you might be experiencing a spiritual low. Don't forget to tend to your energy and soul as you recover from hard times. And don't lose who you are in the process of self-discovery, acquiring wealth, or changing lifestyles. You're expanding, not abandoning your inner self.

TRAUMA RESPONSES

It's profoundly helpful for each of us to realize that everyone experiences instinctive trauma responses. How do you most often react to being/feeling challenged or threatened?

○ **FIGHT:** Facing any perceived threat with aggression + attacking behavior.

○ **FLIGHT:** Running away from the danger and acting in avoidance.

○ **FREEZE:** Unable to move or act against a threat, often disassociating from the moment.

○ **FAWN:** Immediately seeking to please someone else to avoid conflict.

We don't typically have the chance to choose how we respond automatically in the moment, but we can look upon past moments with kindness to our animal instincts.

Consider how you would like to respond the next time you feel threatened . . . and know that it will take practice for you to rewire your response. But with time, you can redirect your response habits. Give yourself time.

SIX OF PENTACLES

Abundance is a state of mind, baby! Whether you are on the giving or receiving end, there's some abundance that wants its way with you right now. Perhaps you need to ask for help—so speak up. You have surrounded yourself with a community willing and able to help you thrive, so let them love you! And if you're the sugar parent on the block, it's time to share those resources. Financial assistance, food, wisdom, creative problem-solving, you name it. This moment is about a flowing energy of exchange, value, and reciprocity (without any sense of "owing," mind you). Gratitude is the way forward.

REVERSED: You're willing to give . . . to an extent. This card is challenging you to be less stingy with your giving. Give yourself a little treat. Then extend care and giving to others.

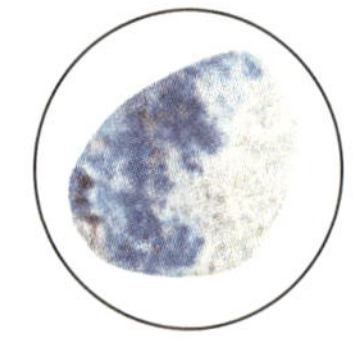

GEM

Lapis lazuli
PROSPERITY, GENEROSITY, EXPANSION

SONG

"With a Little Help from My Friends"
IMAGINARY FUTURE

SCENT

A BAKERY FILLED WITH FRESH PASTRIES

SHARING IN ABUNDANCE

One of the greatest ways to feel powerful is to give a piece of your power to someone who has yet to gain access. What is one space of abundance that you can share with another, and how will you share?

CIRCLE THE AREAS IN WHICH YOUR LIFE CURRENTLY FEELS PROSPEROUS:

REST FUN FINANCES CREATIVITY

FEELING ACCOMPLISHED FOOD AND WATER

COMMUNITY RESOURCEFULNESS SPIRITUALITY

HOME COMPASSION SAFETY WARMTH

PRODUCTIVITY TRINKETS AND BELONGINGS EDUCATION

SELF-ACCEPTANCE ____________________

Fill in the blank with your own

HOW WILL YOU SHARE THIS ABUNDANCE WITH SOMEONE IN NEED?

SEVEN OF PENTACLES

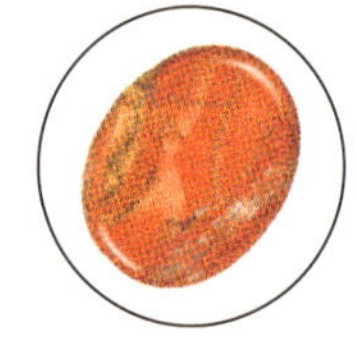

GEM

Jasper
CONTEMPLATION, GROUNDING, CENTERING

SONG

"See the World"
BRETT DENNEN

SCENT

GASOLINE AND BURNT RUBBER

You're killing it! But remember: Slow and steady wins the race. You've been hard at work and your crops are bountiful. Beware of overworking yourself to the point of exhaustion. Though your seeds need nurturing, you won't be able to enjoy the yield if you're too tired to harvest. Pace yourself, take a day off where it's possible (note: we did not say *preferable*), and make sure to tend to your physical wellness. Good things are coming, so stay healthy and ready to welcome them with open arms.

REVERSED: You've invested a lot in something or someone that just hasn't reaped the rewards it once did. Pause and assess how to reconfigure your investments of time, money, and energy so that you get what you want and need.

It's time for a reframing, to reflect on and acknowledge the failures that have served a greater purpose in your life. Failures often teach us more about our skills, needs, and creativity than success ever does. Name three failures that have taught you something or given you clarity to move on from something that no longer serves you, and give thanks.

FAILURE, OUR GREATEST TEACHER

EIGHT OF PENTACLES

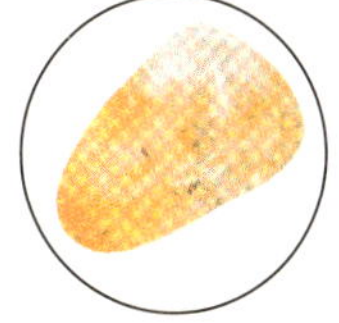

GEM

Citrine
BOUNTIFUL ENERGY, JOY, OPTIMISM

SONG

"Work Bitch"
BRITNEY SPEARS

SCENT

SHAVED WOOD

Repetitive meditation leads to mastery, but the journey can feel tedious. There are always points at which routines begin to stale. No commitment is as great as the commitment we make to ourselves. Visualize a tree growing tall and strong. Without consistent, repetitive watering, the tree cannot grow to its full potential. Be aware of the impulse to abandon something that triggers discomfort. Lean into the anxiety and self-doubt. Trust that this is exactly what you are meant to face in this moment. You will reach your end goal.

REVERSED: You're in the zone for self-improvement. Now is the time to invest in those daily practices that will prove your investment in yourself. A checklist, not perfectionism, is your best friend.

WORK SMARTER NOT HARDER

Try these tips for working smarter, not harder:

- ○ Work in ninety-minute chunks with twenty-minute breaks in between each chunk.
- ○ Schedule your tasks during the day based on how your energy fluctuates.
- ○ Only expect to complete three major tasks a day.

NINE OF PENTACLES

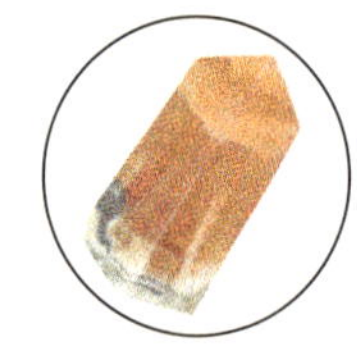

GEM

Honey calcite
HARD WORK, HEALTHY HOME, DEVOTION

SONG

"Love and Peace"
QUINCY JONES

SCENT

FRESH LAUNDRY AND DRYER SHEETS

Everything is aligning and feeling luxurious and abundant! You are doing the things that align with your values, which allows you to prosper in satisfying ways. You are the maker of your destiny. What you choose to do with this life not only impacts your personal outcome, but also that of your community. Using your power—however unimpressive you may think it is—for global good is something you should be proud to claim. When you release yourself from shame, doubt, and undeserved guilt, you inspire others to do the same. Enjoy what you've worked so hard to accomplish. Fly free. Indulge. Thrive.

REVERSED: Do your actions match your values? For example, consider every dollar you have as a vote. Are you investing in businesses, causes, and people you believe in? Go over your actions with a fine-tooth comb and see what's out of alignment.

Name one way you have invested in each of these needs within your home:

- ○ **PHYSIOLOGICAL NEEDS:** ______
- ○ **SAFETY/BELONGING NEEDS:** ______
- ○ **SELF-ESTEEM/LOVE NEEDS:** ______
- ○ **AESTHETIC NEEDS:** ______

AT-HOME NEEDS

TEN OF PENTACLES

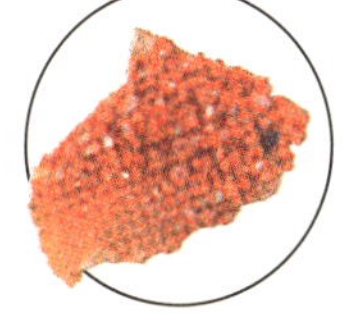

GEM

Vanadinite
BLISS, ABUNDANCE, FULFILLMENT

SONG

"Summer Breeze"
THE MAIN INGREDIENT

SCENT

PIÑA COLADA AND SAND

A cycle of earthly abundance has come to a climactic ending where you find deep stability, success, and attainment. Fortuity encourages us to consider that when everything is in alignment, we are able to find more abundance, more success, more gain. This card indicates monetary and holistic security, speaking to the treasures of earthly life and our ability to find them, give them value, and protect them. When you look at the joy within your home (and bank account), consider all that went into your achievements and this celebration. This is a moment to bask in gratitude.

REVERSED: Time to reassess where you place value in your life. While this reversal may appear to be surface level—about financial or home stress—it's also about the underlying cause of our distress. Ask yourself: *Am I focusing on something that helps me or hurts me? What is the solution here?* (Often, the solution is to ask for help!)

SHARE THE WEALTH

You've mastered a skill and are basking in the glow of your abilities. Now is the time to share the wealth. Where is one place you can volunteer your skills to help someone else? Research one organization you can gift money to in support of their mission—share the organization on social media or with friends.

APPRENTICE OF PENTACLES

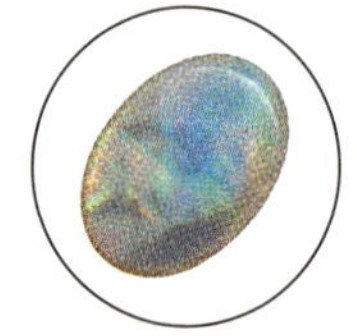

GEM

Opal
SUPPORTIVE, KIND, UPLIFTING

SONG

"Strange Girl"
LAURA MARLING

SCENT

A DEWY, MOSSY REDWOOD FOREST FLOOR

Those who embody the Apprentice of Pentacles work away in the background on significant projects, methodically mastering their chosen craft. Channel this Apprentice for their industrious fertility in the realms of home, work, spirituality, and finances. Tend your garden, cultivate abundance. If you've lost touch with your own body, mind, and emotions, dedicate some time to meditating on how you might best plant new seeds to grow these parts of yourself.

REVERSED: Procrastination is causing you to feel stuck and stale. A new perspective is available if you're open to it. The failures of the past are merely lessons, well-processed fertilizer for whatever projects, hopes, or dreams you seek to bring to fruition. Plant yourself in a new beginning and trust that the soil is nutrient-dense because of what has come before.

GROUNDING FOOT SCRUB DIY

Ground yourself to reconnect with *you*. Honor your hard work with this earthy foot scrub. With all the ways that others depend on you, those feet can feel worn and tired. Replenish.

- ◯ **FOR THE SALT SCRUB:** Mix 1 cup Epsom salt with ¼ cup olive oil or almond oil, 10 drops of tea tree essential oil, and 5 drops of cedarwood essential oil. (In a pinch, peppermint and lavender oils are also great!)
- ◯ Soak feet in a warm water bath for five minutes.
- ◯ Pour out or drain the water bath and massage the salt scrub mixture onto your feet in a circular motion.
- ◯ Add fresh warm water to the bath and soak your feet for another five minutes.
- ◯ Dry off, moisturize, and thank the earth for its grounding spirit.

CHAMPION OF PENTACLES

GEM

Epidote
GROUNDING, DEDICATION, LOYALTY

SONG

"Joy"
KADHJA BONET

SCENT

TEA TREE OIL

The line between dedication and stubbornness is fine. It's the space in which this Champion seeks balance. You may find yourself inspired, but also constricted and obsessed with sticking to one path, one direction, one outcome. Do you feel like you have the sovereignty to choose your own path? Acknowledge the urges that rise and fall as you move forward. Addictive and obsessive tendencies are normal. Detach shame from these waves of impulse. As urges pass by, remain dedicated to your path. The Champion lives within you, steady and joyful in their loyalty to self.

REVERSED: Feeling unable to break through? You may find yourself wanting to blow up anything mundane right now, but it's not the time to try something new. Dig deep and follow through with whatever's getting under your skin. Instead of abandoning a task or routine, release your frustration with a primal howl—then get back to work.

QUIET GUIDANCE

Need a little more guidance in your decision-making? Discover your inner knowing using a pendulum. If you don't have access to a pendulum, use a necklace or attach a crystal to a chain. You can also thread string through a nut or an acorn. Hold your pendulum over this pendulum board and start swinging. As you watch the direction of the swinging pendulum, you will find your answer.

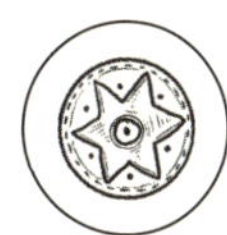

ORACLE OF PENTACLES

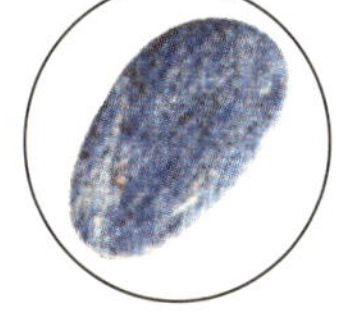

GEM

Sodalite
LOVE, FOCUS, INTUITION

SONG

"Crowded Table"
THE HIGHWOMEN

SCENT

A BOUQUET OF WILD THYME, HONEYSUCKLE, AND LEMONY GERANIUM

Fertility abounds and abundance meets you with ease. The Oracle of Pentacles is a magnet for a bountiful harvest. This energy is down-to-earth, grounded, and knows boundaries. You may be experiencing a flux of material wealth, success, or love, but that doesn't give you permission to overindulge. Discern when to invest, when to spend, and when to be more conservative with your resources. This is also a card of nurturing and striking a work-life balance.

REVERSED: Life is a little out of whack and some tenderness is in order. Are you spending too much time at work or perhaps not enough? Something needs some love. It's time to mindfully look at what's going on and offer yourself some inner parenting. This card sees your strength, ability, and worthiness.

CONNECTING WITH MOTHER EARTH

Spend time with nature's mothering spirit:

- ◯ Take a walk and collect flowers for a wild bouquet.
- ◯ Take one of your regular indoor tasks outside.
- ◯ Find a local source for honey! Local honey is said to help with inflammation and allergies caused by plants in your region.

ELDER OF PENTACLES

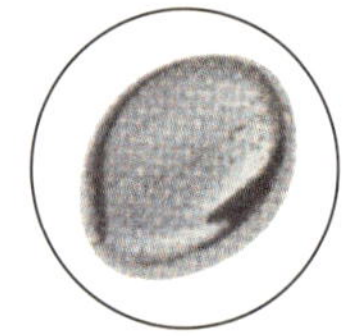

The Elder of Pentacles represents all the worldly success and material abundance we crave. A fatherly figure who builds personal value by accumulating wealth of all kinds, he shares his wisdom with others. To build an empire, you need self-discipline. You've got to believe you deserve it and put in the time and effort to make it happen. Be methodical in your plans. Now is a great time to look to other leaders in your field for guidance. Building on the wisdom of others will increase the value of your own ventures.

REVERSED: You may be in a state of abundance right now, which is something to celebrate, but don't go blowing all your success only to end up back where you started: Review how you are managing your wealth, in all its forms. Be sure there is respect for anything gained so it can remain steady in your care.

GEM

Hematite
STEADY, GROUNDED, ENTREPRENEURIAL

SONG

"Game Winner"
JOEY DOSIK

SCENT

COFFEE GROUNDS

NAME A CAREER/EDUCATION GOAL THAT SEEMS OUT OF REACH:

List three actionable steps to get you closer to your dream. It's okay if you don't get anywhere near the goal yet—each completed action is another leap toward your goal.

1.

2.

3.

CREATING A PRACTICE THAT WORKS FOR YOU

Divinity is not found in perfection. Rather, it's found in persistence, devotion, and our drive for fulfillment. Divinity is found in our constant pursuit of beauty, knowledge, community, and creativity, and in every obstacle we encounter along the way. To err is human—and to be human? That's sacred.

This is all to say that it's okay if your pursuit of tarot—or any mental health or spiritual practice—isn't perfect. You may forget to pull a card even if you have every intention of creating a daily ritual. You might let your altar gather dust. That tarot deck you thought would be the perfect fit may end up sitting on the shelf, unshuffled, forever in stasis. And that's okay! The cards—and the wisdom of the universe—aren't ever waiting on you. They're just hanging out, ready when and if you are.

To create a practice that works for you, consider if you're good with structure. Moorea feels invigorated by creating detailed structure, while Callie needs freedom to check off her to-do list in a more creative flow. We have very different practices in all things, including tarot. While Moorea enjoys connecting with her tarot deck each morning and peacefully documenting the process, Callie keeps several decks on her desk and chooses to pursue readings at random intervals, whenever the mood strikes. For us, these systems work because they feel sacred in ways *we* find important. Maybe you identify with Moorea's desire for devoted contemplation, or perhaps you like Callie's ever-unfolding conversation with her cards. You're allowed to like both . . . or neither. Find a ritual that works for you.

A tarot app on a smartphone might be a good way to get started, while some might love the thrill of trying many different decks. Keep a deck by your bedside table, and if you're new to tarot, we recommend keeping a tarot journal so that each reading becomes tangible. Create a social media profile or a scrapbook to document your readings. What do you desire from your practice? How might you support this desire, given your tendencies and circumstances?

How you choose to integrate tarot into your life will change over time, too. If you're pulling a card each morning, you likely want to keep an eye out for how that card shows up throughout your day. You might end each day by journaling. If you're doing full spreads about certain topics, you may set reminders in your phone with notes about your readings. Callie likes to pull twelve cards at once annually (usually on New Year's

Day or her birthday)—one for each month of the coming year—and take notes on the reading to consult throughout the year for insight, guidance, and inspiration. Finding ways to make tarot work for you will make it more engaging and satisfying.

To elevate something from a habit to a ritual, consider what carries meaning for you. Sometimes the simplest way to create a ritual is to light a candle or some incense before beginning a task. You may choose to speak your intentions aloud, which is a common practice in both ancient and modern religions—in some pagan practices, it might be called spellcraft, while in Christianity it's called prayer. Whatever you call it, create a ritual that bears meaning for you.

SOME OTHER SUGGESTIONS:

- ◯ *Set up an altar (see page 149).*
- ◯ *Choose a symbolic time of day to pull cards.*
- ◯ *Intentionally prepare food and/or drink ahead of readings.*
- ◯ *Create boundaries around your practice (i.e., you may not want others to touch your tarot deck, or you might only read for yourself—whatever feels right for you).*
- ◯ *Burn meaningful incense or scented candles. (Make sure whatever you burn is done safely and ethically. We encourage our fellow white practitioners to avoid white sage and palo santo, as these are endangered and sacred to Indigenous peoples. Some safe, accessible alternatives include rosemary, cedar, rose, and lavender.)*
- ◯ *Join a group practice either online or in person.*
- ◯ *Pay professionals for readings as a part of broadening your education and studying how others practice.*

We encourage you to create your rituals and continue them fearlessly. Your practice is yours to mold. It's also yours to protect, uphold, and defend. Treat it as you would any soft, newborn thing. Hold it gently and keep it safe. You deserve this space to expand, and only you can give it to yourself.

OUR WISHES FOR YOUR HERO'S JOURNEY

We hope this book and the *Every Little Thing Tarot* inspire you to make space for your most expansive self. Consider this your permission to take the space you need *and* to take up space. And remember that the hero always returns to the same place it all began in the first place: the self.

We wish you the most thrilling, beautiful adventure, and a safe journey home.

With deep love and gratitude,

Callie Little Moorea Seal

CALLIE LITTLE AND MOOREA SEAL

The Major Arcana and The Hero's Journey
The Fool
The Magician
The High Priestess
The Empress
The Emperor
The Hierophant
The Lovers
The Chariot
Strength
The Hermit
The Wheel of Fortune
Justice
The Hanged One
Death
Temperance
The Devil
The Tower
The Star
The Moon
The Sun
Judgment
The World

RESOURCES

BOOKS:

- ◯ **HOLISTIC TAROT: AN INTEGRATIVE APPROACH TO USING TAROT FOR PERSONAL GROWTH** by Benebell Wen
- ◯ **MASTERING THE TAROT: BASIC LESSONS IN AN ANCIENT MYSTIC ART** by Eden Gray
- ◯ **MODERN TAROT: CONNECTING WITH YOUR HIGHER SELF THROUGH THE WISDOM OF THE CARDS** by Michelle Tea
- ◯ **QUEERING THE TAROT** by Cassandra Snow
- ◯ **SEVENTY-EIGHT DEGREES OF WISDOM: A TAROT JOURNEY TO SELF-AWARENESS** by Rachel Pollack
- ◯ **TAROT AND DIVINATION CARDS: A VISUAL ARCHIVE** by Laetitia Barbier
- ◯ **TAROT FOR CHANGE: USING THE CARDS FOR SELF-CARE, ACCEPTANCE, AND GROWTH** by Jessica Dore
- ◯ **TAROT FOR THE HARD WORK** by Maria Minnis
- ◯ **TAROT FOR YOUR SELF: A WORKBOOK FOR PERSONAL TRANSFORMATION** by Mary K. Greer
- ◯ **THE LIBRARY OF ESOTERICA: TAROT** by Jessica Hundley

DECKS:

- ◯ **EVERY LITTLE THING YOU DO IS MAGIC TAROT** by us—Callie Little and Moorea Seal
- ◯ **DUST II ONYX: A MELANATED TAROT** by Courtney Alexander
- ◯ **MYSTIC MONDAYS TAROT** by Grace Duong
- ◯ **OUR TAROT** by Sarah Shipman
- ◯ **PAGAN OTHERWORLDS TAROT** by Linnea Gits and Peter Dunham
- ◯ **QUEER TAROT** by Ash + Chess
- ◯ **THE SOMNIA TAROT** by Nicolas Bruno
- ◯ **TAROT OF THE DIVINE** by Yoshi Yoshitani
- ◯ **THE LIONESS ORACLE TAROT** by Alejandra Luisa León
- ◯ **MODERN WITCH TAROT DECK** by Lisa Sterle
- ◯ **THE RAINBOW TAROT** by Sonia Lazo
- ◯ **THE WILD UNKNOWN TAROT** by Kim Krans
- ◯ **WILD MESSENGERS ALCHEMICAL TAROT** by Lola Pickett, edited by Callie Little

WEBSITES AND APPS:

- ◯ biddytarot.com
- ◯ labyrinthos.co
- ◯ thetarotlady.com
- ◯ Golden Thread Tarot app
- ◯ #SelfCare app by TRU LUV Inc.

Callie Little (SHE/THEY) is a multidisciplinary artist and writer whose work has been featured in *Cosmopolitan*, *Architectural Digest*, *Teen Vogue*, *Vice*, *The Establishment*, *Harper's Bazaar*, and many other fine publications. Her podcast, *The Pocket Coven*, is internationally ranked and her artwork has been shown in galleries throughout the Pacific Northwest. Find her at @goshcallie and callielittle.com.

Moorea Seal (SHE/THEY) is an artist, designer, and writer. Her bestselling list-making journal series, *The 52 Lists Project*, includes six guided journals for mental and emotional well-being for adults and children. She is also known for her home décor book, *Make Yourself at Home*. Her books have been published in several languages and have sold over one and a half million copies worldwide. Find her everywhere at @mooreaseal, and shop her fine art, home goods, and more at mooreaseal.com.

Callie Little

Thank you to . . . Moorea, for being my soul sister, dear friend, and perfect partner for this project, and for bringing it to our agent, Lindsay Edgecombe, whose hard work, grounded support, and enthusiasm have been a balm each step of the way. Our first editor, Sara Neville, whose excitement and care got us started, and our final editor, the Virgo oracle Sahara Clement whose easeful professionalism, warmth, and joyful collaboration took us to the finish line. Our incredible designer, Danielle Deschenes, who met us with generosity, added pure genius to our vision and created these truly stunning products. Our team at Clarkson Potter, and our agency, Levine Greenberg Rostan. Thank you to Bobi Blue, Ron Knight, Aimie Kiang and Bryce Cohan for being the first to believe in me. My family: Amber Huntsman, the greatest surprise who has been with me in every life, to the Littles, Woolfs, Kilburns, Ally Koff, and Mirabai Starr. Luanne Wilson and Kirill Glushko for telling me I can do hard things and sharing a home with me for the entirety of this project. Candace DesBaillets for being the most unflappable friend a girl could have, Ariel Henley and Jennifer Borges Foster for celebrating with me from a place of knowing, Mint Siegel for being a constant source of light, my studio mates Emily Rose Lumsdaine, Jac Milliron, and Ames Delgado for being so supportive and inspiring, Victoria Sass for making my collaborator the happiest I've ever seen, Kelli Gordon for my sanity. Megan Falley and Melissa Sussens for helping me learn to balance the tinsel with the trees. Finally, to the one who chooses me every single day, who gave me a last name and a family, who loves every part of me and lets me love them back with everything I've got, Cee Little.

Moorea Seal

First, I would like to acknowledge that while writing this work, Callie and I lived on the traditional land of the first people of Seattle, the Duwamish People past and present. We honor with gratitude the land itself and the Duwamish Tribe. I also acknowledge and honor the Suquamish Tribe, past and present, and their traditional land where I now live and create. Thank you to Callie, my dear friend and co-author who has celebrated me through some of the wildest shifts in my adult life. Years of writing, researching, and making art together has woven the coziest blanket around our sisterhood. Thank you to Lindsay Edgecombe for being our champion. Your belief in our creative work as individuals and co-authors has been our driving force. Thank you to Susan Roxborough for being the link between my past and present that connected us to Sara Neville. To Sara N. and Sahara Clement, our dynamic duo of editors, your wisdom has sharpened our work into the glistening jewels we now treasure. Danielle Deschenes, you've understood our vision from day one, have been so gracious in creative collaboration, and have transformed our aesthetic dreams into design realities. Cee Little, thank you for the steady love and belief you've always held in abundance for Callie. To Kelli Gordon for giving name to my life experience, and Jodi Palmer for guiding me through the forest. Thank you to Ms. Conte, Mr. Baxter, Laura Lasworth, and every teacher who guided my younger selves to communicate through artistic expression. And to Vic Sass, my love, the person who wooed me by delivering me home grown strawberries in bed and reading me excerpts from *Tarot for Change*, you have my heart. With yours tethered to mine, every ounce of life is magic.

THIS BOOK AND ITS CORRESPONDING TAROT DECK ARE INTENDED FOR ENJOYMENT AND PERSONAL ENRICHMENT ONLY. THEY SHOULD NOT BE USED IN PLACE OF PROFESSIONAL SUPPORT, NOR ARE THEY INTENDED TO DIAGNOSE, CURE, OR ALLEVIATE ANY AILMENTS OF THE BODY, MIND, SPIRIT, OR CIRCUMSTANCE.

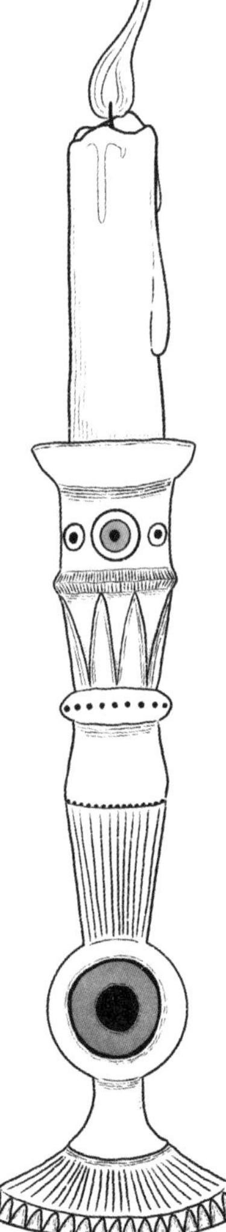

Published in the United States by Clarkson Potter/Publishers, an imprint of the Crown Publishing Group, a division of Penguin Random House LLC, New York.
ClarksonPotter.com

CLARKSON POTTER is a trademark and POTTER with colophon is a registered trademark of Penguin Random House LLC.

Library of Congress Cataloging-in-Publication Data is available.

ISBN 978-0-593-58030-1

Printed in China

Editor: Sara Neville and Sahara Clement
Designer: Danielle Deschenes
Production editor: Serena Wang
Product[illegible]nager: Jessica Heim
Copye[illegible] | Proofreader: Katy Miller
Mark[illegible]

10

First Edition